Evangelistic Sermons

Evangelistic Sermons

By

J. W. PORTER

Editor "Western Recorder"

NEW YORK   CHICAGO

Fleming H. Revell Company

LONDON   AND   EDINBURGH

New York: 158 Fifth Avenue
Chicago': 17 North Wabash Ave.
London: 21 Paternoster Square
Edinburgh: 75 Princes Street

AFFECTIONATELY

DEDICATED

TO ONE, WHO IN SUNSHINE AND
SHADOW; THROUGH GOOD AND EVIL
REPORT, LOVED AND TRUSTED ME—

MY MATCHLESS MOTHER

Foreword

THE author of these sermons is widely known for his many labours in the Kingdom of Christ. He has wrought as pastor, editor, and evangelist. He occupies to-day one of the strongest pastorates among Southern Baptists; and along with its many exacting labours edits a paper of large influence and distinct leadership. Besides these serious tasks he finds time to do much evangelistic work beyond his own pastorate. The discourses in this volume have been forged out of an intensely busy life and out of a heart kept warm by constant connection with the throbbing issues of life. No one knowing the author would expect anything but vital orthodoxy from him. This collection of sermons will disappoint no one in that respect. Sin and salvation, the two great themes of the New Testament, are set out clearly and strong by our preacher in the pages following. It is worth while for our leaders, pastors, editors, and teachers to study and practice the finest of all ministerial arts, the art of winning souls to Christ. Dr. Porter has done well to take time out of his otherwise busy life to do the work of an evangelist. The future of Christianity is wrapped up in aggressive, orthodox evangelism. Nothing can take its place. The contagion of soul-winning will help every department of Christian service. It gives me peculiar pleasure to commend these sound, sensible, evangelistic discourses for what they are and because they come from the heart and brain of one of our busiest workers, who is equally set for the defense and the propagation of the Gospel. My fervent wish is that the readers of the book may be many and that the Word of the Lord as set out here may run and be glorified.

REV. J. B. GAMBRELL, D. D.
Southwestern Baptist Theological Seminary,
Fort Worth, Texas.

Contents

I.	Sin	.	.	.	.	.	9
II.	The Question and the Answer	.				.	18
III.	Lot's Escape from Sodom	.			.	.	27
IV.	Come!	.	.	.	.	.	38
V.	Salvation by Grace	.			.	.	46
VI.	The Will	.	.	.	.	.	56
VII.	Not Ashamed	.		.	.	.	66
VIII.	The Banquet of Death	.			.	.	76
IX.	The Fool	.	.	.	.	.	83
X.	Backsliding	.	.	.	.	.	92
XI.	Repentance	.	.	.	.	.	102
XII.	Past Feeling	.	.	.	.	.	113
XIII.	Faith	.	.	.	.	.	121
XIV.	A Pilgrimage	.	.	.	.	.	133
XV.	Prayer	.	.	.	.	.	142
XVI.	Heaven	.	.	.	.	.	150

I

SIN

Fools make a mock of sin.—PROVERBS 14:9.

SIN is not a theory, but a stubborn and tragic fact. It is a condition that confronts us from the cradle to the grave. Our conception of sin determines our opinion of the Cross. Given one's views of sin, we have his idea of the atonement.

The Cross was predicated and predetermined on account of the nature and character of sin. Some one has suggested that sin can be cured by an operation. The heart, and not the head, is the seat and citadel of sin. Only a change of heart can make us a new creature in Christ Jesus and save us from the penalty of sin.

Fools make a mock of sin in their idea of sin. It is becoming quite common to regard sin as a mistake. Sin is infinitely more than a mistake, it is a cruel crime. We can apologize for a mistake, but we must expiate a crime.

Sin has blinded our eyes, until we have become spiritually colour-blind. Our constant exposure to sin deadens our spiritual sensitiveness. Truly it has been said:

" Vice is a monster of so fearful mien,
   To be hated needs only to be seen,
   But seen too oft, familiar with her face
   We first pity, then endure, and then embrace."

Sin is sin, under all conditions and circumstances. No condition can justify wrong, or cancel the guilt of sin. In the rich and poor, wise and foolish, sin is essentially the same. Some seem to hold the view that education will atone for sin. Education can never atone for sin, though it may enlarge and intensify the power of sin. The schoolroom can never take the place of the Cross, higher critics to the contrary notwithstanding. Whether clothed in rags, or broadcloth, sin is ever the same. The flash of the diamond will not atone for the hell in the heart.

There is only one quality of sin. The variations of sin are in quantity, and not quality. In essence sin is ever and forever the same. The difference is in degree, not in quality. Sin is sin, whether in an angel by the throne of God or in the harlot in the brothel.

Poor McCullough went from the stage to a sanitarium for lunacy. Gazing through the iron bars, he would say: "I am not mad! I am not mad!" But he was.

Fools make a mock of sin in their practice of sin. Men try to differentiate between "big" and "little" sins. The smallest sin, if unforgiven, will damn the greatest soul. The smallest grain of sand will disarrange the mechanism of the finest watch. It is the little microbe that brings death to millions. It is,

"Little drops of water,
    Little grains of sand;
    Make the mighty ocean,
    And the pleasant land."

The little sin of to-day means the big sin of to-morrow. We do not start great sinners. The unregenerate grow in iniquity as the regenerate grow in grace. The man becomes a gambler by degrees. It is not uncommon to hear one speak of "small vices," and yet these vices point the path to perdition. In the day of judgment no sin will appear small! Record, conscience and God will one day reveal every sin in its true light.

Fools make a mock of sin by denying they

are sinners. We have all sinned and come short of the Glory of God. We were conceived in sin and shapen in iniquity. Through the Federal Headship of Adam we come into the world in a state of condemnation. We may have never committed any great outbreaking sin, and yet we are all guilty before God. A rattlesnake is a rattlesnake, whether he ever bites any one or not. His bite is only a manifestation of his nature, and the poison he vomits in the veins of his victim is a part of his being. It may be truly said of one and all—

" Poor worm of the dust,
  Dearly ye pay for your primal fall,
  A few flowerets of Eden, ye still may inherit,
  But the trail of the serpent is over them all ! "

Heredity constitutes us sinners, and even the best environment, without Christ in the heart, but intensifies and develops our sinful nature. And while we are all sinners, thank God, many of us are sinners saved by grace. We become so accustomed to sin that we forget our sins, yet if our sins are not forgiven, the recording angel keeps the record, and will not forget them. Many of the sins of our youth were long ago forgotten. Well has one prayed,

"Lord, remember not the sins of my youth against me." The forgotten sin does not mean the forgiven sin; and if unforgiven, the sin of the long gone years will yet confront us. God spare us from having to face our long accumulated catalogue of crime!

One day a man was gazing upon the old gallows, at Fort Smith, Arkansas, while the hangman was telling him of the many criminals who had been hanged there. While listening to the grewsome story, a mockingbird lit upon the gallows, and began its gladsome song. All unconscious, the feathered songster, of the tragedies that marked with melancholy the sad and lonely spot. So we forget the sins that have wrecked and ruined the lives of others, and making fast for our own destruction.

Whatever we may think of sin, it is exceedingly sinful, because it is destructive. Sin is the universal destroyer. The real tragedy of life is the wreck and ruin which sin hath wrought. Sin has shed rivers of blood and tears, and marred and murdered the lives of millions. The insanity of sin leads to soul-suicide, the outstanding crime of all the centuries. The lost man crimsons his hand in the blood of his own soul. Sin incited the mob that murdered Christ, and drove a God to an earthly grave. And yet in spite of our sin, Christ loves us, and yearns for our salvation. Some years since, in Louisville, Kentucky, a father sent his little daughter to the saloon to purchase beer. Accidentally she spilled some of the beer. Already crazed by drink, he began whipping her, because a part of his beer was gone. While brutally beating her, she said: " Papa, don't kill me, I didn't go to do it. Papa, I love you." Though sinners nailed Him to the Cross, He said, " Father, forgive them, for they know not what they do."

Sin is exceedingly sinful, because God hates it. " Do I not hate the abominable thing saith the Lord." Surely, we can ill afford to love what God hates. We rightly hate lying, stealing, and murder, and yet these crimes are but sin in action. Sin is the father of every unkind word and evil deed. Sin knows no pity and shows no mercy. It blights the life of the manliest man, and withers the being of the most winsome woman. It corrupts governments; bankrupts the home, and deluges the world with the blood of its own citizens.

Sin is God's worst enemy and Satan's greatest ally.

Either the righteousness of Christ or the sin of Satan must conquer in every life. Sin, like the sinner, " stoops to conquer "; and, if cherished, will one day conquer. We often rest in fancied security that we can control our sins, when we are being mastered by them. The eagle swoops down upon the unsuspecting serpent and buries his claws in the quivering flesh. With the wounded serpent he flies upward, far upward till he is lost in the blue of the sky. Soon he is seen slowly descending. His wings are weary and his flight is heavy. In a moment, like a leaden ball, he dashes dead to earth. In the hour of his seeming victory the poison of the serpent has conquered.

Sin is the more unpardonable, because God has provided a pardon. In its last analysis, all sin is willful. The unregenerate man is a lost sinner because he prefers the pathway of sin. " Whosoever will " may come and be saved, and whosoever will may refuse to come and be lost. Thank God, grace is greater than sin and the blood of Jesus Christ His Son cleanses us from all sin.

" What can wash away my sin
Nothing but the blood of Jesus,
What can make me whole again,
Nothing but the blood of Jesus.
For my cleansing, this I see,
Nothing but the blood of Jesus;
For my pardon this my plea,
Nothing but the blood of Jesus."

Oh, that to-night you might seek safety from
the guilt and power of sin.   Perhaps, at this
moment, the destiny of your soul trembles in
the balances.   You cannot afford to take the
risk.   On one occasion, Major Penn, of blessed
memory, urged upon his hearers the necessity
of an immediate acceptance of Christ.   He
closed his great discourse with these words,
" You cannot afford to take the risk."   At
midnight he was hastily summoned to the bedside of a dying girl.   He entreated her concerning her soul.   In response to his request
that she accept the Saviour, she said: " Major
Penn, it is more than kind of you to come and
try to help me, but it is no use.   To-night when
you said, ' You cannot afford to take the risk,'
I wrote on the fly leaf of the hymn book, ' I
will take the risk.'   You will find the book on
the left hand side of the church, as you enter,
and on the third pew.   I took the risk, and in

a little while I will meet my God unforgiven.
Good-bye, Major, go help others.   I am lost."
He went out and it was night.   In a little while
she was face to face with Him, with whom we
all have to do!   God help you to be ready,
when that hour shall come!

II

THE QUESTION AND THE ANSWER

What must I do to be saved?—ACTS 16: 30.
Believe on the Lord Jesus Christ.—ACTS 16: 31.

IT is worthy of note that this is the only instance in the Bible in which a penitent sinner asked of an inspired apostle the terms of salvation, and to which he received a direct reply and was then and there saved. This being true, we can surely afford to rest the salvation of our souls upon the plan of salvation as established by this example.

Salvation is a comprehensive term, but in this instance its meaning is restricted to the forgiveness of sins. There were many things the jailer would, and doubtless did as a saved man, but his inquiry was concerning the salvation of his soul from the guilt and penalty of sin.

The question is the more impressive and the answer more conclusive in the light of the surrounding circumstances. The scene was laid at midnight in a Philippian prison. Paul and Silas had been imprisoned for preaching the blessed Gospel of the Son of God. Instead of bemoaning their fate, at the lonely hour of midnight, they were singing praises to God and rejoicing in the fact and fellowship of suffering—

"And prisons would palaces prove,
If Jesus would dwell with me there."

Unheralded, the mighty earthquake comes, and the walls of the prison are shaken, and the doors are thrown open. The jailer, realizing that his life would be forfeited, should the prisoners escape, fell trembling at the feet of Paul and Silas. With death staring him full in the face, he looks to Him from whom cometh all our help, and, thank God, he looked not in vain.

We should, one and all, ask this question, because the soul is *immortal*. Immortality would dignify a dog and make the humming-bird worthy of ceaseless study. The fact that man is immortal makes him, under God, the rightful master of the universe and the final explanation of the crucified Christ. Even our Saviour could not afford to die for something doomed to extinction. Death is too dear a price to pay for anything that is not deathless. The longing for immortality has been found among all the nations of mankind. Not only is immortality an innate concept, but man is conscious of immortality. There is not one here to-night who is not conscious of the fact that somewhere his soul shall live forever. The flowers that bloom in beauty about us, the grass that grows green in the summer's sun, are but splendid prophecies that, though we die, we shall live again. " Where shall I spend eternity? " becomes, therefore, the question of all the centuries. We must spend it somewhere. Shall it be in heaven or hell? Christ died that we might spend eternity in our Father's House. The story is told of a mother who, with her little babe, started for a neighbour's home. Overtaken by a blinding snow-storm, she lost her way, and far in the night found herself freezing. Forgetful of self, she looked to the life of her child. Taking off her own clothing, she wrapped it about her child—

" She stripped her mantle from her breast,
    And bared her bosom to the storm,
    Then sank upon the snow to rest,
    And smiled, to think her babe was warm."

The following day her lifeless body was found, but the little child was alive. The Son of God died that we might live! Oh, riches of grace in Christ Jesus!

We should ask this question because by nature and practice we are *lost*. Not, as commonly affirmed, that we will be lost if we die in our sins, but lost this very moment if we are out of Christ. " He that believeth not is condemned *already,* because he hath not believed on the only begotten Son of God."

Salvation or condemnation is the present possession of every accountable soul. He that believeth on the Son *hath* eternal life, he that believeth not is already condemned. Let not the poor lost soul delude itself with the thought that it is not yet lost, but rather let it realize that it is already in a state of condemnation, which death may, at any moment, transform into damnation. Only the sinner, saved by grace, can sing:

> " Amazing grace how sweet the sound;
> That saved a wretch like me;
> I once was lost, but now am found,
> Was blind, but now I see."

In spite of abounding grace, the unregenerated soul is lost, without God and without hope in the world! And yet Christ died to redeem his undying soul. The story is told of a misguided girl who was enticed from her home into a life of shame. Her father, hearing that she was in a distant city, went in search of the poor prodigal daughter. Walking through the red light district, now and then he was heard to cry, " Shoba." Street urchins gathered about him and called him crazy. A policeman approached him and inquired what he meant by " Shoba." He whispered his sad story to the listening officer. Though hardened by many stories of sin and sorrow, tears stained his cheeks as he said: " Go on, old man, and say that as much as you like." Sending the boys away, he walked with the broken-hearted father. As the old man again cried, " Shoba," it was heard, and a girlish face looked from the window, and in a moment a weeping girl threw her arms about her father's neck. That night the train bore father and daughter to the old home amid the hills of New Hampshire. " Shoba " was the sheep call, and in the days of childhood's innocency she would cry " Shoba," and the sheep would come and eat from her tiny hands.

In spite of sordid sin and deep disgrace, Christ calls us back to our Father's home.

The answer is as clear and simple as it is possible for human speech to make it—believe on the Lord Jesus Christ and you are saved.

It is worthy of note that Paul did not tell him to do anything but simply to believe something. We are not saved by anything we can do, but by what Christ has done for us. We cannot pay the debt of sin, and fortunately for us, Christ has already paid it, and we have only to accept by faith the receipt He so freely offers. All that separates a sinner from Christ is a lack of faith in Christ. A man is not damned for what he does, or fails to do, but for what he fails to believe. The plan of salvation, by grace through faith, is seemingly the simplest that God could have devised for a lost and ruined world. It is one of the few things that is capable of universal acceptance.

Even the untutored savage or the most ignorant little child has known and practiced something of faith.

It cannot be explained, though it may be illustrated. Christ Himself never explained the plan of salvation. When Nicodemus asked an explanation of the mysteries of the new birth, Christ merely illustrated by the way of the wind, " The wind bloweth where it listeth, but ye know not whence it cometh or whither it goeth."

The father challenged the faith of the child

when he said, " Throw your doll in the fire and
I will buy you a nicer one." The child hesi-
tated for a moment, and then her faith in
father triumphs, and she consigns the old toy
to the flames.

We are saved through faith only. It is not
faith plus or minus, but faith alone. It is not
faith and works, lest any man should boast,
but " by grace are ye saved through faith, and
that not of yourselves; it is the gift of God."

There are degrees in faith; and while one
is saved with an everlasting salvation, the moment he believes he should grow in grace and
faith. Christ said of the Centurion, " I have
not found so great faith, no, not in all Israel."
That faith is capable of expansion is evidenced
by the prayer of the disciples—" Lord, increase
our faith." The question for the unforgiven
sinner is not how much he is trusting Christ,
but is he really trusting Him for his soul's
salvation.

Can you say:

> " My hope is built on nothing less,
> Than Jesus' blood and righteousness.
> I dare not trust the sweetest frame
> But wholly lean on Jesus' name."

There are those, too, who have faith and

yet lack the full assurance of faith. They are continually harassed with doubts, yet in spite of their doubts and fears, in their deepest soul are trusting Christ for the forgiveness of their sins. Nor does doubt preclude the fact of faith.

Thomas doubted, yet he was, nevertheless, a true disciple. It is our duty, however, to cultivate our faith and not our doubts. While our doubts may not discredit us, certainly they add nothing to our credit.

Job had faith, but after his sore affliction he entered into the full assurance of faith.

> " I know that my Redeemer lives,
>   And ever prays for me:
> A token of His life He gives,
>   A pledge of liberty."

Nearing the end of the earthly journey and sustained by an unfaltering faith, Paul could say, " I know him whom I have believed, and am persuaded that he is able to keep that which I have committed to him against that day."

If we have faith in Christ we *shall* be, not may be, saved. Salvation is more than a mathematical certainty to every one who trusts in Him who is abundantly able and willing to save. He who trusts the Saviour is not saveable but saved. His feet are on the rock of ages; his brow above the clouds.

May the God of all power give you grace to trust Him just now.

A young lady who had come forward for prayer was asked by the preacher why she could not accept the Saviour. She replied, "I cannot believe." The preacher then inquired if she could not believe the Bible. She said, "Of course I believe the Bible." "Do you not believe that Christ died to make possible your salvation?" asked the preacher. Her prompt answer was, "I know He did." She finally admitted her trouble was that she could not trust herself. Christ does not wish us to trust in ourselves, but in Him who died to redeem us from all iniquity.

Believe on the Lord Jesus Christ and be saved with an everlasting salvation; fail to believe on Him and be damned with an everlasting damnation!

"Halleluiah, 'tis done, I believe on the Son;
   I am saved by the blood of the crucified one!"

III

LOT'S ESCAPE FROM SODOM

*Escape for thy life, look not behind thee, neither
stay thou in all the plain, escape to the mountain lest thou be consumed.*—GENESIS 19: 17.

THE ancient City of Sodom has been
rightly considered one of the world's
most wanton and wicked cities. The
record of its sin has been perpetuated in the
laws of nearly every land. Its iniquity was
so monstrous and enormous that God decided
upon its speedy destruction. It is only a question of time when all sin and unrepentant
sinners will be destroyed. Lot and his family
had left the country for the city. In fact city
folks are country folks moved to town. He
had been made a Judge, and his wife, doubtless, occupied high social position, and it was
likely due to the love of the sinful city that
caused her death. Some of us, through pain-
ful experience, can answer to the lines, "Is
this vile world a friend to grace to help me on

to God?" Lot's own life had not been
blameless, since he "pitched his tent towards
Sodom," yet the Lord loved him and sent an
angel to warn His servant, Lot, that the city
was doomed to speedy destruction. God often
warns us of impending peril, and it is our duty
to give heed to the warning. Alas, how frequently we have neglected the solemn and
timely warning. The Scottish chief might
have saved his army had he heeded the warning—

"Lochiel, Lochiel, beware of the day,
  When the Lowlands shall meet thee in battle
    array.
  For the field of the dead rushes red on my
    sight,
  And the clans of Culloden are scattered in
    flight."

His foolish reply was:

"Go preach to the coward thou death-telling
    seer," etc.

Some of the most tragic failures of history
might have been avoided had the warning voice
been heard. Cæsar was warned against attending the meeting in the Forum at which he
met his death. The warning went unheeded
and he met his death in the place he made im-

mortal.   Pilate was warned against taking part in the death of Christ and his destiny was sealed by an ignored warning.   Jackson and Walling, a few days before they murdered Pearl Bryan, attended a meeting in Cincinnati conducted by Moody and Sankey.   Had they listened they might have heard the voice of God and turned from their devilish designs. They despised the warning and died a felon's death.

The red buoy not only marks the channel but serves as a danger signal to the mariner.   The breakers pay no attention to the buoy.   From the cradle to the grave, through all the centuries, God has been urging men to flee from the wrath to come.

God's voice will be heard; for every knee shall bend and every tongue confess His name. England laughed at the warning voice of Patrick Henry when he made the famous declaration, "Taxation without representation is tyranny, and resistance to tyrants is obedience to God," they counted it but the utterance of the schoolboy-orator.   But England did hear him.   The nation heard him, in the thundering of American cannon; in the groans of their dying, and read his message in the blood of their gallant dead as it crimsoned American soil. The Sodomites likely laughed at Lot, for he had often warned them of the consequences of their sins. Perhaps they counted him cranky, yea, even crazy, in his zeal for their lost souls. It may be that there is some one here to-night who has had his last warning. Would that I could say something that might stop you in your mad career. A watchman kept at a bridge that spanned a deep canyon along a mountain railway, saw the bridge swept away by the mighty flood. In less than two hours the midnight train would come thundering by. Taking his red lantern, farther down he crossed the canyon on a footbridge and walked up the track to meet the coming train. In a little while he heard the rumbling of the fast-flying train. In a few moments the headlight flashed its flood of light upon the rails. He waved his red lantern to stop the train. No answering whistle comes from the engineer. For some reason his warning signal has not been seen—on it comes, speeding its way to destruction. Stepping off the track, his fevered brow fanned by the flying monster, he throws his lantern full in the face of the engineer, and shouts aloud—" For

God's sake, stop!" Your home, the church; your many friends, join in the cry of the hurrying angels as they cry, "For God's sake, stop." Would that I could say something that would cause you to halt before it is everlastingly too late!

The purpose of their escape was that their lives might be saved. We all rightly love our lives. Even the condemned criminal hopes for his life.

> "The wretch condemned with life to part,
>   Still, still, on hope relies,
>   And every pain that rends the heart,
>   Bids expectation rise."

Some years since I was holding a meeting with Dr. John D. Jordan in the First Baptist Church of Decatur, Illinois. Pacer Smith, a professional baseball player, had been sentenced to be hanged. The sheriff of the county requested us to speak with him concerning his soul, stating at the time that he had refused to talk with any preacher. I visited him in person and tried to point him to the Saviour. He emphatically said that he did not care to discuss the subject; and we turned sorrowfully away. At the request of the sheriff I was present at the hour of execution. When he had mounted the scaffold the sheriff told him of our presence and that he would gladly give him time to talk with us about his soul. Again he refused. The black cap was adjusted, and as the trap was sprung, he cried, " Jesus, have mercy." With a wild wail, his soul went out to meet its maker. In spite of foolish boasting, men do crave life, and without Christ dread the hereafter. It is not only death that is dreaded, but the destiny of the soul. " Where shall I spend eternity," like Banquo's ghost, will not down at our bidding. There are but two homes for the soul, one is heaven, the other hell. Your conscience tells you which would be your home, were you to die to-night. There are those, to be sure, who claim that there is no such place as hell. They even laugh at the minister who warns against this terrible place. Their real objection is not to the preacher but to the Bible. The New Testament tells us there was a man who " lifted up his eyes, being in torment." If eternal punishment is not true, then the Bible is untrue and altogether unworthy of belief. He who rejects the fact of hell must likewise reject the fact of heaven, and to reject these is to discredit Christ and reject the Scriptures. Sometime since a scoffer

said to me, " In the course of time the fires
of hell would have to burn out." I reminded
him that we had positive proof of the fact that
Vesuvius had been burning for about two thousand years, and that the probability was much
longer. And just here I offer it as my deliberate opinion that I never knew a man who
did not believe in hell that was not traveling the
path that led there. It is more or less natural
for one whose life logically leads to eternal
punishment to deny eternal punishment.

Not only was Lot and his family told to
leave the sinful city, but even warned not to
look back in their flight. Many start for the
Kingdom but pause and look back to the
cherished haunts of vice. Like Lot's wife,
speedy destruction comes upon them while they
linger to look upon sinful scenes. Perchance
you are bound to some habit from which there
seems no deliverance. You have earnestly
striven to break the claim that binds you, but
all in vain. Poor Prometheus was bound to
the rock while the vultures gnawed away his
vitals. By and by the unseen angel strikes the
chain and Prometheus is free. Christ stands
ready to-night to sever the chain that binds you
to some besetting sin. Oh, that you might

come out from the unspeakable slavery of sin
into the glorious liberty of the Gospel of the
Son of God. Would that I could shout aloud
till all the children of men would hear,
" Escape for thy life, look not behind thee,
escape for thy life, lest thou be consumed."
Oh, forget not—

> " There is by us a line unseen,
> That crosses every path
> The hidden boundary between
> God's patience, and God's wrath."

Lot was commanded " neither stay thou in
all the plain." Many try to stand midway
between the domain of God and Satan, and are
lost by sinful hesitation. There is no such
thing as " No Man's Land " in the spiritual
realm. We are, one and all, at this very moment either in the Kingdom of God or Satan.
We are saved or lost. We are friends of
Christ or enemies of the Cross. Many are
halting in the valley of decision. Multitudes,
multitudes in the valley of decision! At this
moment you may be fighting a mighty battle
in your mind. You are struggling with doubts
and darkness. Oh, that you would give Christ
the benefit of the doubt—"All my doubts I
give to Jesus." How can you doubt Him who

through the centuries never forsook a friend
or broke a promise? It was the damning
doubt whispered by the accursed Tago that
murdered the innocent and forever wrecked
a home. Your doubts may decide your destiny and separate you forever from the Lord.
Stay not in the plain; but flee to the mountains,
where there is joy and life and peace and
safety forever and forever! Perhaps you are
looking at your own merits instead of the
merits of Him who died to redeem you. It is
not a question of your being good enough but
of Christ being good enough to pay the penalty
of your sin. It is not what you have done or
can do, but what Christ has done for you.

> " Jesus paid it all,
> All to Him I owe;
> Sin had left a crimson stain,
> He washed it white as snow."

Let us look not at ourselves but to the everlasting hills of God, from whence cometh all
our help. Not that we are worthy, but "worthy
is the Lamb, to receive riches and honour and
glory and power now and forever."

Surely God has given sufficient warning and
he that is lost can only say, Amen! to his own
condemnation. You have been warned times

without number. From childhood to this good hour the warning voice of God has sounded in your ears. You have traveled a pathway blocked with prayers and made slippery with the tears of your loved ones. A narrowly averted accident; a burning fever; the funeral procession along your street; or the casket within your home may have all been solemn warnings to your sinful soul. Your warning may come as it came, in vision, to America's most gifted poet, when it is too late to escape—" Quoth the Raven, ' Nevermore.' "

I give it as my deliberate conviction that had I not accepted the Saviour when I did I would have died a stranger to grace. The soul has its hour and its crisis. You have your chance; will you crucify it? This moment of mercy is yours, will you murder it? Surely,

> " There is a solemn murmur in the soul,
>   Which tells of the years to be,
>   As sailors hear the billows roll,
>   Ere they reach the sea."

On the morning following a storm two boys found a little boat stuck fast in the sand. They tried hard to float it but failed. They waited a few days when the highest tide of the season would come. When the tide had reached its crest, with a long pole against the boat and pushing with all their might and main, one of them cried—" Go out, old boat, it is the highest tide you will ever know." Time and tide are alike in your favour to-night. Will you launch out on the blessed sea of His boundless love!

> " There is a tide in the affairs of men,
>   Which if taken at the flood,
>   Leads on to fortune."

I call to witness this great congregation; I call to witness the disembodied spirits of the deathless dead; I call to witness the angels of God; I call to witness the Christ that was crucified for you, that I have faithfully warned you of the peril of your soul. " Escape for thy life, look not behind thee, neither stay thou in all the plain, escape to the mountains lest thou be consumed! "

IV

COME!

*'And ye would not come unto me that ye might
have life.*—JOHN 5 : 40.

MAN wandered away from God, and
not God from man. Adam turned
the Garden of Eden into a mighty
gulf, that separated him and his posterity from
God and righteousness. This great gulf Christ
bridged with His own bruised and bleeding
body, thus making possible the way home.

Through the long weary years the attitude
of God is echoed in the word " Come," that of
man in the word " Go." A compelling Christ
and a repelling creature make up the tragic
story of human history.

The clear and emphatic teaching of the text
is that Christ *wishes us to come.* He does not
mock us in our sin and misery. It is man,
not God, that delights in man's undoing. God
delights not in the death of the wicked but re-
joices in the presence of His angels over one
sinner that returns. The sinner can never ex-

perience the joy in coming home that Christ feels in welcoming him home.

He wishes us to come as we are.

The sinner must come to Christ with his sins, and be saved by Christ from his sins. If one can get rid of his sins without Christ then there is no need of his coming to Christ. The condition of the prodigal would have remained unchanged as long as he remained in the far country. It was when he reached home that he was fed and clothed. Christ came to call, not the righteous but sinners to repentance. We may thank God that we were lost sinners, that we might become sinners saved by grace. Our very debasement made possible our eternal exaltation.

" Come Great Deliverer, Come."

He wishes us to come now.

Christ makes no promise to the lost sinner for to-morrow—to-day, if you will hear His voice, harden not your heart. He deals in the ever-living, eternal present. All the years that are past were once the present, and all the years that shall be must become the present. Now is the accepted time and now is the day of salvation.

Sometime since I visited a man who was dying in a hospital, away from his family and without hope and without God, requested the privilege of talking with him concerning the salvation of his soul. With all possible politeness he suggested that I wait until to-morrow. The following day I called and he begged me to excuse him on account of nervousness. As I left him he made me promise to " return to-morrow," and whatever his condition he would have me talk with him about his soul. According to his promise, I called the next day, but his body was at the morgue, his soul in eternity.

> " Trust no Future, how'er pleasant
> Let the dead past bury its dead!
> Act,—act in the living Present
> Heart within, and God o'erhead."

There is nothing to be gained, and everything to be lost by delay. Procrastination is not only the thief of time but of eternity.

> " Year after year it steals,
> And to the mercy of a moment leaves,
> The vast concerns of an eternal scene."

The highway of the years is strewn with the wreck of splendid purposes, the kindly word that was never spoken, the generous deed that was never done.

There be few who do not hope, some day, to seek and find the Saviour. Yet with many the " convenient season " never comes. Those who thus determined to defer are unwilling to fix a date, however near or remote, when they will surrender themselves to the Saviour. Apparently they wish to enjoy the pleasures of sin to their dying day, and then turn to a neglected and outraged Saviour. It is difficult indeed to believe that any one could reject a proffered Christ if he could only realize the sacrifice Christ has made for the salvation of the soul.

Many years ago, in the outskirts of London, a little gypsy boy heard Mr. Sankey sing, and only as Mr. Sankey could sing:—

" But none of the ransomed ever knew
How deep were the waters crossed ;
Nor how dark was the night that the Lord
    passed through
Ere He found His sheep that was lost."

When he had finished the song and was making ready to leave the little boy touched him and said: " Mister, won't you sing again about the sheep that was lost? " The great singer sang again the verse, and putting his hand on the gypsy boy's head said: " Goodbye, my boy, may the Lord bless you." Many years after a world-famous evangelist visited America and called at the home of Mr. Sankey, who was then aged and blind. After making himself known, the gypsy boy of long ago who had been led to Christ by the Gospel sung by Mr. Sankey requested that he sing to him again. He sang to him again that song. Looking heavenward with his sightless eyes, the aged singer in Israel sang and sobbed:

" But none of the ransomed ever knew
   How deep were the waters crossed;
   Nor how dark was the night that the Lord
      passed through
   Ere He found His sheep that was lost."

Then together, Ira D. Sankey and Gipsy Smith bowed and thanked God for the infinite redemption through riches of grace in Christ Jesus.

" Oh, why do you wait, dear brother,
   Why do you tarry so long?
   Your Saviour is waiting to give you
   A place in His sanctified throng."

He wishes us to come that we may have life.
Surely there can be no greater gift than eternal life in a passing and dying world.

Death is the world's most frequent, yet least familiar, visitor. There is not a name represented here but a great majority of those who have borne it have not long since left the scenes of life. There is not a home in all the land that is not allied by death to the " faraway home of the soul."

Some years since I visited the home of my friend, Henry Schmelz, a millionaire banker of Hampton, Virginia. He showed me through his home, on which wealth, art and culture had exhausted themselves to enrich and beautify. Finally he unlocked a door, and with eyes streaming with tears, his mighty frame shaken with emotion, with trembling voice he bade me enter. Composing himself, he said: " This room is practically as my wife left it when she went to be with her Saviour. The world calls me rich, and some, perhaps, may have envied me my fortune, yet I would give every dollar I have to see her again in that chair."

In vain we sigh for the " touch of a vanished hand, for the sound of a voice that is still."

We may go to live forever with our loved ones, but they cannot return to share the fleeting days with us.

Yes, die we must, and die we will, but **in** Him, thank God, we die to die no more. **We** are all traveling to the land of shadows, but many, let us hope, through the shadows to the realm of endless day. The snows of the silent centuries may fall upon our forgotten graves, but the call of the Christ shall be heard in caverns of clay, and a glorified body, formed in the image of the changeless Christ, shall yet be ours.

When the rivers shall no longer run to the sea and the tide shall cease to ebb and flow; when the stars shall no longer shine and the sun go out in unending darkness, our souls shall live with Him who is life and light and love forevermore.

" They tell me of a city far up in the sky—
   I want to go there, I do;
   It is built in the land of the sweet bye and bye,
   I want to go there, don't you? "

Oh, that you would come! Christ wishes you to come with all your sins, and come now that you may have everlasting life. If you fail to come the blame is all and only yours.

The papers recently contained the account of a man who took his own life by jumping into the bay. A man on the wharf threw him a rope that fell within a few inches of his hands. Instead of seizing the rope he deliberately pushed it away and went down to a watery grave. To-day Christ throws out the life-line that every sinful sinking soul may be saved with an everlasting salvation! Seize the life-line and Christ will draw you to Himself!

V

SALVATION BY GRACE

For by grace are ye saved.—EPHESIANS 2:8.

THE greatest word in all the languages of earth is the word grace. It means undeserved favour, unmerited mercy; yea, in its last analysis, everything for nothing. The partakers of grace know its meaning, yet even they have never fathomed its unbounded depths or scaled its immeasurable heights. Paul, in describing and glorifying grace, refers to it as " free " grace. Grace is the only thing in all the world that is absolutely and universally free. Grace is the only possible way of salvation. The sinner is dead in trespasses and sins. A dead man can do nothing to give himself life, nor can the hand of man do aught to help him. He is dead, and if he receives life it must come from above and come as a gift. Only two plans of salvation have ever been proposed. God's plan is salvation by grace; man's plan is salvation by grace and good works. Though numberless denominations, there are only two systems of theology. One glorifies God, the other glorifies man. There are only two classes that seek the Saviour. One says, " Jesus paid it all, all to Him I owe." The other says, " Jesus paid a part and only a part to Him I owe." In salvation it is either God or God and I. Christ's atonement was either complete or incomplete. If complete, it does not have to be perfected by man. If incomplete, then it must be perfected by man; and hence Christ and man make a joint atonement for sin. In other words, the merits of the atonement must rest in man, or Christ, or in man and Christ. Sad to say, a mistake concerning the plan of salvation may be the price of the soul. We may err in many things regarding the Scriptures and yet be saved; but if we commit our souls to any other than the Scriptural plan of salvation, by grace, we are lost. It matters not how honest one may be in his opinion concerning the plan of salvation. It is not a question of his honesty, but of the truth of Scripture. One may drink carbolic acid honestly, believing that it is something else, but his honesty will not prevent his death. It would be better if we were dishonest in our belief of error, as there would be a greater chance of coming to a knowledge of the truth.

Many years ago Dr. Baber, of Georgia, 'phoned a prescription to a druggist with directions how it should be taken. The druggist replied that he could not fill the prescription as directed by the doctor, as it would kill the patient. The doctor resented the action of the druggist and told him that he would come in person and fill the prescription. Having compounded the prescription, the doctor said, " Now to convince you that I know a good deal more about medicine than you do, I will take a dose of it." The druggist begged him not to do it, telling him that it would undoubtedly kill. The physician took the medicine and was dead in a few hours. A few days later a physician who was a friend of the lamented doctor visited his office. Noticing an open book on the desk, he saw marked the formula that had resulted in the death of his friend. The printer had made the mistake that cost a good man his life. Dr. Baber was entirely honest in his opinion, but his honest conviction did not prevent his death. Our honesty can never become a satisfactory substitute for truth.

Whatever the future may bring forth, His grace will be sufficient. The way may be dark and the path rough, but as thy days so shall thy strength be. Many have lived in bondage for fear of death. They have longed to be willing to enter the Valley of Shadows. They have longed for dying grace before the dying hour. This God has not promised, but He has promised that His grace shall be sufficient, and His grace can make a dying bed " as soft as downy pillows are." I have seen the dying saint as he stepped in the cold waters of the River of Death and with a smile on his lips leave the shores of time—His grace was sufficient.

Some one had said that it took him fifty years to learn three things. First, that he could not save himself; second, that Christ did not wish him to save himself, and, third, that Christ had already provided for his salvation, if he would only believe it. A helpless babe on the railway track in front of the fast-flying train seems doomed to speedy death. Just before the deadly engine reaches him a kindly hand snatches him from the jaws of death.

Surely in after years the child could claim no
credit for escaping death. That we are this
moment out of the abode of the damned is due
solely to the grace of God. Hence it is that we
can sing with truth,

> " Oh, to grace how great a debtor,
>   Daily I'm constrained to be,
>   Set thy goodness like a fetter
>   Bind my wandering heart to thee."

Dr. Townsend, who has made an exhaustive
study of the word " charis," says it retains its
Old Testament connotation of finding favour,
but that it also reveals signs of Greek influence. It means good-will, bounty, and denotes
favours bestowed. The New Testament use
of the word " grace " is clearly that of unmerited favour and undeserved kindness and
mercy. And while it is true there is nothing
freer than sovereign grace, and less expensive
to the recipient, it is also true that there is
nothing that has cost God more. When we
consider the cost of the riches of grace we
readily see the price paid to make grace a
gracious fact would, had it been possible, have
impoverished God. Grace is the price of
blood, and the blood of a God-man. Our debt
of sin was paid with the blood of Christ, and

the culmination of Calvary was riches of grace in Christ Jesus. And just here comes the age-long battle between Christianity and legalism. This battle was waged in the first century of the Christian Era, and has continued with un-abated fury till this good hour. Judaism was legalism, pure and simple, and legalism is the antithesis of the Gospel of grace.

There is probably no better illustration of the wonderful working and application of grace than is seen in the life and death of the dying thief. This experience is such an ob-jective manifestation of the grace of God in Jesus that we stand silent before its unfathom-able reality. Our Lord's authority to forgive sins on earth, to seek and to save and welcome the most depraved of men in the name of God, is magnified on the Cross. It was out of an experience, equally vivid in its way, that Paul was led to exalt the depth of the riches both of the wisdom and knowledge of God, and to praise the glory of His grace, which He freely bestowed on us in the Beloved. When we reach heaven and home at last and look back over our imperfect lives and see the wounds that sin has made that grace might be effective and free we will cry, " Honour and glory, not unto ourselves but unto Him who loved us and gave Himself for us!"

The parable is a divinely intended demonstration of the greatness of grace and the wideness of His mercy. In the parable of the Great Supper, God prepares the supper and invites the guests, utterly regardless of their social or moral standing. In the parable of the Prodigal Son, he who had sinned grievously against his father was freely forgiven and gladly welcomed to his father's house. He who was legally " dead " was made " alive" and restored to his place in his father's house. As Forsyth says, " Christ was God's act of grace and did not merely announce it." From the beginning God's grace was prompting His action in Christ, whose will was making the same grace real and available for men. It flowed through His personality and rose as a tide to its flood at the Cross.

The parable of the Debtors illustrates and emphasizes operative grace. Here the amount forgiven becomes, in some sense, the gauge of gratitude. It is difficult to conceive of one being forgiven, and yet refusing to forgive. Grace not only causes our forgiveness but causes one to forgive others. " There is such an intimate reciprocity between divine and human forgiveness that our Lord represents them as the objective and subjective aspects of Christian experience."

Salvation by grace is the only plan of salvation, of possible universal application. Any mental or financial qualification could not be all-inclusive. Only a Gospel of grace can be preached "to every creature." In the glories of this great grace, the thief, the harlot and the murderer may have a part. The Pharisees, as their spiritual progeny, objected to the Saviour eating with the publicans and sinners.

Grace presents the only effective way of salvation. If one is saved by law he would be lost by the slightest infraction of the law. We are told that by the deeds of the law no man can be justified; and what the law could not do grace has done and can do. Christ is the end of the law to every one that believeth. The law, like the poisoned shirt of Nessus, means death to all that it embraces.

If saved by good works, a cessation of good works would necessarily mean a cessation of salvation, and hence the inevitable destruction of those who trust in them. It is but fair

that if we are saved by good works we should
be damned by bad ones.   It is not of works
lest any one should boast, but by grace through
faith are ye saved, and that not of yourselves,
it is the gift of God.   We work from the Cross,
not to the Cross.   In other words, we work
because we are saved and not that we may be
saved.   It may be replied that this doctrine
discounts the worth of good works.   Nay,
verily, to the contrary, the man who realizes
that within himself there is no merit and that
he owes eternal life to the goodness and grace
of God will be all the more anxious to live
and labour for Him.   We certainly would be
inclined to do more for one to whom we owed
all than to one to whom we owed only a part.

> " Jesus paid it all,
>   All to Him I owe;
>   Sin had left a crimson stain,
>   He washed it white as snow."

If Christ saves us He not only deserves but
must have the credit for our salvation.   Our
God is a jealous God and will share His glory
with no one.   Christ must be all or not at all.
If we knew that our tongue was soon to be
paralyzed and we could choose the last word

we should ever utter, that word would be
" Grace ! "

> " Through many dangers, toils and snares,
>   I have already come ;
>   'Twas grace that brought me on thus far
>   And grace shall lead me home."

VI

THE WILL

Turn ye, turn ye, for why will ye die?
—Ezekiel 33:11.

ON first sight, the question seems altogether superfluous. That all men must die is a fact ordained of God, and well known to man.

The cemeteries of the centuries; the multitude of the ages, that are now no more, confirm the tragic fact that it is appointed unto all men once to die. It is said that the eyes of Xerxes, as he looked from his exalted throne over his vast army, were filled with tears. To one of his courtiers, who inquired the cause of his weeping, he replied: "As I gaze on this mighty throng, the thought comes that in less than one hundred years all will have gone the way of the earth."

And still the old sexton rings:

> "Gather them in,
> Gather them in."

How true

" The leaves of the oak and willow will fade,
Be scattered around and together be laid,
And the old and the young,
And the low and the high,
Shall moulder to dust, and together shall lie."

Our text, however, has no reference to man's mortality, but rather to the death of the soul.

The will is alike man's greatest asset and liability. Our will makes us responsible creatures. God Himself respects the human will. The lack of a rightly exercised will power is responsible for many of life's failures. This is often illustrated by children of the same parents. In the same family are two boys; one of them may be handsome, polite, honest, pleasing and pious. The one thing that is lacking is a strong will. He is minus a propeller, and drifts upon the sea of life. The other may be uncouth, homely and with less of mental power, yet he has an imperial will. With him, failure is only an incentive to greater effort. Nothing can daunt his deathless determination to succeed. He goes onward and upward and leaves his impress upon his age. " I will " descends into the deep and brings to view the hidden pearl. Like a swift-winged angel, it cleaves the blue, and sails above the clouds. " I will " mounts up with eagle wings, till it bows before Him who is not only the " Great I am," but the " Great I will."

And just here it may be well to note the difference between one willing something, and being willing to something. Pilate was willing to release Jesus, but he did not will to release Him. You may be perfectly willing for the Church to prosper, but do you will that it shall prosper?

Every rejection of Christ is a willful rejection. The man who refuses the offers of mercy refuses them willfully. Neither condemnation nor justification is an accident, but the result of a willful acceptance or rejection of Jesus Christ.

A sinful and stubborn will keeps many from the Saviour. It is tragically true that by refusing, or failing to rightly use the will, we may lose the power to will. The will unused for the Master may become incapable of use for the Master.

Sin is a disease that weakens the will as well as the body. There is such a thing as spiritual as well as physical paralysis. Both body and will may be paralyzed. The hand that is not lifted for a long period of time will never be lifted again. The will that remains unused for Christ may one day be incapable of willing for Christ. Not long since I prayed with a man who was addicted to drink. In parting, I urged him to look to the Lord and use his will power. His sad response was, " I have no will, and am as powerless as a child to resist the temptation to drink." The poor opium eater really desires to conquer his dreadful habit, but he depends on a will that has already been wrecked. Oh, that such an one might look to Him from whom cometh all help.

Mr. Moody urged a man to come to Christ. He replied, " My sins hold me like a chain." " Then," said Mr. Moody, " come with your chains." God help you to will to come to Him with all your sins and be saved from your sins.

Then why will you die? Is it because you cannot understand the plan of salvation? It is true you can never understand the process of redemption, but you can understand enough to be saved, with an everlasting salvation. We may state the plan of salvation, but we cannot explain it. Even Christ never explained the plan of salvation. Happily for us, Christ does not require us to understand how His blood cleanses our souls from sin, but only believe it. Faith, and not knowledge, is the conduit that conveys the cleansing power. The child cannot understand what the father does, but it can trust him to do what is best. Even as the child permits the mother to put it to bed in the dark, so we may follow blindly, if needs be, where He leads the way.

Certainly you do not understand the crime you commit in rejecting Christ. There is, perhaps, not one here that would not gladly accept Christ if he could but realize what is involved in rejecting Him. It is not my invitation that you reject, but the invitation of Him who died to redeem you. The preacher is called of God, and commissioned by Christ to bid you come. Could you but understand the awful guilt incurred in resisting the Holy Spirit you would accept Him now. After the close of the first day's battle of Gettysburg, in the twilight, two men met who had been separated from their companies. One wore the blue and the other wore the gray. Their ammunition being exhausted, each seized his sword and with parry and thrust began a battle of life and death. Soon one plunged his sword into his opponent's breast and, pushing him down, pinioned him to the earth. The dying man, looking into his face, recognized him and cried, "My God, Father, you have killed your boy." Oh, if the father could only have known, his sword would have never been unsheathed. Could you only understand the exceeding sinfulness of sin, you would this moment seek the Saviour.

Can it be that you believe you are not included in the warning words of our text? Is it possible that you are haunted with the fear that salvation was not intended for you? "Why will ye die" means why will you die? Christ commanded His disciples to preach the Gospel to every creature. Some one has surmised that Peter protested when the Master said, "Preach the Gospel to every creature." "Can it be," Peter might have well replied, "that we are to preach forgiveness to the sinners at Jerusalem?" In tones of infinite tenderness the Saviour says: "Go preach it to every creature." "But, Lord," answers Peter, "surely we are not to preach forgiveness to the man who drove the nails in your hand." In accents of undying love, the Crucified replies, "Go preach it to every creature." For the spear He offers the sword of the Spirit; and for

the crown of thorns He offers a crown of life.
Christ says, " Whosoever " will, may come.
It may be that John, on the lonely Isle of Pat-
mos, protested as the Lord continued His all-
inclusive invitation.   " Write," said the Lord,
" and the Spirit and the bride say, Come."
We may well imagine John saying, " Now,
Lord, is not the invitation sufficient? "   That
it may be the more emphatic, the Lord says
write, " Let him that heareth say, Come."
Well might John reply, " Surely the invitation is all that any one could desire."   " But
make it yet more gracious and glorious and
let him that is athirst come."   " Enough, Lord,
let us place the seal on the last message of
mercy to man."   " No, make it as high as
heaven; as wide as earth's remotest bounds,
and say whosover will, let him take of the
water of life freely."

Oh, that like the Prodigal, to-night you
might say, " I will arise and go to my father."
It was not sufficient that the Prodigal was
sorry that he left home and had wasted his
heritage and himself in riotous living.   It was
necessary that he return to his father's house.
You must not only be sorry for your sins, but
sufficiently sorry to turn to God, through Jesus

Christ your Saviour. God says, "In the day of my power I will make them willing," but we must be willing. No one can be saved against his own will. Should God permit you to enter heaven in spite of your unregenerate heart and stubborn will, you would, if possible, leap over the walls of the city, whose Builder and Maker is God, to find the home of your soul amid the horrors of hell! Should you at last lift up your eyes, being in torment, you can reply to the question of our text, " I am here because I preferred the path, and willed the way, that led to this dreadful abode." Christ willed to die that you might will to live.

It takes courage to will for Christ. There should be no cowardice at the Cross. When Christ was suffering the unspeakable cruelties of Calvary His enemies cried, " Come down from the Cross." We thank God to-night that He did not come down, but died at duty's door. Through the ages rings the chorus of the imps of darkness, " Come down from the Cross." To the man or woman who desires to live an upright life comes the deadly whisperings of the Devil, " Come down from the Cross; don't get too good; come and be as others." To turn a deaf ear to the voice of the multitude

requires the highest possible type of courage.
Many a man who has unflinchingly faced the
deadly cannon has surrendered without even a
struggle to some temptation.   Many of our returning soldiers will come with scars on their
bodies received in honourable conflict and some
of them doubtless with scars of sin on their
souls.

Oh, for the courage to stand alone, if needs
be, against our best friends.   Public opinion is
a changing quantity.   The same mob that cried
" Hosannas," later shouted " Crucify Him."
The mob is as fickle as it is false.   Evermore
it is true:

" Once show the world that you feel afraid of
　　its bark,
　And it will fly at your heel,
　Fearlessly face it, it will leave you alone;
　But it fawns at your feet, if you fling it a bone."

Many years ago, shortly before my visit to
Nanimo, British Columbia, there was an explosion in one of the coal mines.   More than one
hundred and fifty lost their lives in the terrific
explosion.   Those who survived the awful
crash rushed to the exit of the mine that they
might be taken up to safety.   The cage was
going up for the last time, and all were on, and

the signal given to hoist the cage. It was found that the cage could not ascend owing to the number crowded in it. One man jumped off and said, " I will stay and die; I have no wife or children dependent on me." Immediately another jumped off and said to the other, " You must go and I will stay. It is true, you have no family to look to you for bread, as I have; but you are not prepared to die, and I am." He then pushed his friend in, saying, " Go on, and when you reach safety just remember that I died that you might live and have another opportunity to accept Christ, who died for you." With its burden the cage slowly ascended, and all who were in were saved. The hero who gave his place to another was soon consumed by the devouring flames:

> " He gave His life for me,
> His precious blood He shed,
> That I might ransomed be,
> And quickened from the dead."

" Turn ye, turn ye, for why will ye die? " Eternal life and heaven, unending death and hell, warn you to turn and live!

VII

NOT ASHAMED

For I am not ashamed of the Gospel of Christ, for it is the power of God unto salvation, to every one that believeth.—ROMANS I : 16.

SURELY, if any man had a right to be ashamed of the humble beginnings of the Gospel, Paul was that man. Born in a cosmopolitan city, gifted with a great mind, a graduate with honours of the school of Gamaliel, and a religious aristocrat of the strictest sect of the Pharisees, it was but natural that he should cherish pride and despise a self-abasing Gospel. And this leads us to say, the one besetting sin of all the centuries has been pride. Indeed, I am not sure but that it is the fruitful mother of all other sins. Unfortunately, we have tried to Christianize the word and make pride a laudable possession. In tracing the use of this word we find that it is never used in the Bible to denote anything

that is praiseworthy or desirable. In spite of this, it is not uncommon to hear one exhorted to preserve his pride. In visiting the home of one of our members, the lady of the house, who had once been wealthy, remarked, " We are poor, but proud." If she spoke truly, the family possessed a deadly combination and deserved to be pitied. Philip, the father of Alexander the Great, is reputed to have said, " This is the proudest day of my life." Being asked the occasion of his pride, he replied, " On this day my horse won in the Olympian games; Parmenio, my General, won a great victory, and on this day Alexander was born." Obviously it was his horse that won the prize, his General that won the victory, and certainly his wife was due a large share of the credit for the birth of Alexander. Cash, clothes and the cemetery seem to constitute the triune basis for modern pride. The fact one has a plethoric bank account, or possesses a superior wardrobe, or is the descendant of some illustrious sire, is supposed to afford sufficient cause for real and lasting pride. A moment's meditation will reveal how scant the ground for glorying.

Paul was not ashamed, after learning the

" good news," to preach it to others. It is tragically true that shame keeps many a one from Christ and greatly impairs the usefulness of His followers. Through a sense of pride the young woman has preferred to become a crushed flower rather than be called a " wall flower." The young man has chosen the path that leads to the penitentiary that he might be able to gratify the demands of pride. It is probably true that Napoleon's destiny was determined the day he discarded Josephine. Prompted by pride, he put away, perhaps, the only woman who ever really loved him that he might gratify a posthumous ambition. The story is told of a medical student at the University of Virginia whose parents denied themselves all but the absolute necessities of life that he might complete his medical education. The day of his graduation being near, his father wrote him that he would come to see him graduate. Being ashamed of his father, who was both humble and poor, he replied that there would be no use in his coming. Not realizing the motive that prompted his son's reply, he wrote no more, thinking he would give his son a pleasant surprise. On the day prior to his son's graduation he met him and

two other students on the streets of Charlottes-
ville. "How do you do, my dear boy?" was
the affectionate greeting of the poor and aged
father. Ashamed of his father in the presence
of his fashionable companions, he said, "The
old fellow thinks he knows me. Come on,
boys, we've got no time to fool with a crazy
man." The old man, broken-hearted, turned
his steps homeward. In a few days they
buried him on the lonely hillside, his grave
a monument to the false pride of a sinful
son.

Paul was not ashamed to preach this Gospel
in the forum of proud imperial Rome. Full
well he knew that a Cato, a Cæsar, or an Antony
never had such a message as he longed to bring
to the Romans, even those of Cæsar's household. He knew that their Christless civiliza-
tion would lead to destruction without Christ.
And just here it will be well to bear in mind
that a Christless culture is America's greatest
menace. Many schools are attempting to substitute their curriculum for the Cross, and
learning for righteousness. Our universities
are becoming the cradles of a Christless criti-
cism and hotbeds of horrible heresies. Man-
made gods dug the national graves of Greece,

Rome and Germany, and we may well profit by
their example.   Christ is the only salvation of
nations and the only Saviour of individuals.
Though the preaching of Paul was a matter of
small moment to the city, which from " her
seven hills of beauty ruled the world," the
Gospel that he preached is to-day the greatest
factor and power in the universe.   The forum
of Rome is but a shadowy suggestion of its
erstwhile splendour; the Palace of the Cæsars
only tells the tale of decay and departed gran-
deur; the Coliseum is rich only in its ruins and
a mere echo of bygone glory!   Yet the Gospel
that Paul declared continues, and will continue
conquering and to conquer, till the kingdoms
of this world shall become the Kingdoms of our
Lord and His Christ!   Paul was not ashamed
of the *power* of the Gospel.   It is the only
power that can give life to the dead sinner.
Christ had saved him, and he knew that the
same Christ could save others.   Other things
may help, but only the Gospel can save.   Many
things may contribute to our reformation, but
only the blessed Holy Spirit can cause our regeneration.   Human agencies may whitewash
a man, but only Christ can wash him white.
Water will cleanse the body, but it requires the

blood of Christ to cleanse the soul; for the blood of Jesus Christ His Son cleanses us from all sin. It is not only the power to give life, but also to *preserve* life. Christ is not only mighty to save, but mighty to keep! With blessed truth we sing, "Jesus saves, Jesus saves," and may sing, "Jesus keeps, Jesus keeps." With bands of steel He binds us to Himself. A Christ that could only save would be an incomplete Christ; but the Christ that saves and keeps is the Saviour that gives a complete salvation. Not only does it give life, and preserve life, but it is the power that triumphs over death, hell and the grave. Human wisdom makes no reply to death, and speaks no word of consolation at the graveside. It stands dumb in the presence of death, and offers no word of hope for all the eternal years. "I am the resurrection and the life," crowns with glory even the long-forgotten grave. No wonder Paul was not ashamed of the power of such a Gospel. Some day you may see a notice of my death. But say not I am dead, but rather that I have crossed the river of death, on the bridge of faith, leaning on the everlasting arms. The Gospel is the only full and final answer to the question, "If a man die shall he live again?" We are born to die, but we are born again to live forever with the Lord!

> "We are going home, we are going home,
> We are going home to die no more."

Paul was not ashamed of the *scope* of the Gospel. It is to "every one" that believeth. To the banker and his bootblack, the Queen and her washerwoman, to the Chinaman and American, to the rich and poor, the wise and foolish, this Gospel brings the same message of hope and life. All human systems are exclusive rather than inclusive. Their glory is not so much what they include as what they exclude. A diamond is deemed precious by its owner not only because he has it, but because others do not have it. If diamonds were as plentiful as brick no one would care for them. Thank God, salvation is offered free to all for the asking. No man, or set of men, can get a corner on grace, or secure a monopoly of the Gospel. Of all trusts, the ecclesiastical trust is most to be dreaded. The Gospel is to "every creature." It was sufficient for those who crucified Him. To the man who placed the crown of thorns upon His brow; to the man who drove the nails in His hands, and to the man who plunged the spear in His side.

> " Was it for crimes that I have done,
> He groaned upon the tree;
> Amazing pity, grace unknown,
> And love beyond degree."

The mother whose daughter had been lured from her home and into a life of shame vainly sought her daughter. At the suggestion of a well-known detective, the mother gave him one of her pictures. He told her that her picture would be placed in some of the lowest dives, with the hope of the daughter seeing it. Underneath the picture were the words " Come home." One night, in a city many miles from the old home, the picture was placed in a public dancehall. A girl entered the dancehall, and seeing the picture, fell fainting to the floor. The same night a train bore the girl and the detective towards the home of her youth and innocency. In palaces and huts, in churches and in dens of vice, the Son of man has placed His likeness with extended hands, pleading with us to come to Him and be saved with an everlasting salvation.

Paul was not ashamed of the simplicity of

the Gospel. To every one that believeth. It is at the very simplicity of the Gospel that many are mystified and misled. Like Naaman, had we been told to do some difficult thing to get eternal life, we would, perhaps, have readily attempted it. The Gospel of Christ is not the power of God unto salvation to every one that worketh, or that feels good, or does good, but to every one that believeth. This plan of salvation may seem easy, and it is, but it was hard enough for Him who made it easy for us. Salvation, being conditioned on faith, is made possible to all. Had it been made possible by money or knowledge, however little the quantity of either, many would have been excluded, but every accountable person can believe. In this, as in all things, God has manifested His infinite wisdom and goodness. Some one may say, "If I could only see my way clear, I would gladly accept Him." We are not saved by "seeing our way clear," but by believing on the Lord Jesus Christ; for "by grace are you saved through faith, and that not of yourselves; it is the gift of God."

The engineer, speeding through the midnight darkness, at best can see but little of the way. As the engine advances the shadows lift and light falls upon the way. Moment by moment and step by step God will show us the way.

Is it because you are ashamed of the Gospel that you will not come to Him now?

> " Ashamed of Jesus, can it be
> That mortal man's ashamed of Thee? "

With broken will and humbled heart, throw yourself prostrate at His feet. The Saviour is not ashamed of you; why should you be ashamed of Him?

VIII

THE BANQUET OF DEATH

Belshazzar, the King, made a great feast to a
thousand of his lords, and drank wine before
the thousand.—DANIEL 5:1.

BABYLON was one of the world's most
renowned and beautiful cities. It was
the most strongly fortified city of all
time. The walls surrounding the city were
three hundred and fifty feet high, and broad
enough at the top for horses and chariots to
travel with safety. Enough of provisions were
stored in the city to withstand a siege of twenty
years. For further security, there was a
spacious tunnel under the Euphrates, through
which soldiers might pass in case of an emer-
gency. The Hanging Gardens of Babylon
were known as one of the Seven Wonders of
the World. They were built by the King for
his Queen to remind her of the home of her
youth and compensate for the barren country
about Babylon.

In this city of unsurpassed beauty and luxury the King made a great feast that was attended by a thousand of his lords, their wives and their concubines. Not even the Arab will pitch his tent among the ruins of the once glorious city. In spite of the wealth and strength of this wicked city its glories have long since gone; its splendours long since perished.

Gaiety was the first course in this banquet of disaster and death. Like many others, they believed a banquet impossible without strong drink. Naturally, they wished to deaden their consciences for the orgy in which they were engaged. Liquor is the natural ally of vice, as it hushes, for the moment, the accusing conscience and makes sin a pleasure for a season. As we now look back over the landscape of years, blighted by blood and tears and broken hearts caused by strong drink, we are astounded that our nation so long permitted this inhuman curse. If our nation now had all the money liquor has cost it there would be quite enough to pay every dollar of indebtedness caused by the last war. The poor drunken husband, from whose eye a tear dropped in the glass of water being held to his lips by his wife, said to his evil companions, when asked to drink, " No, I have been drinking my wife's tears long enough." There is nothing so insidious as strong drink. It comes in the guise of friend, and ere its purpose and power is realized its victims have become helpless slaves. Even the wild eagle gives his scream before he seizes his victim; the ferocious tiger gives his growl before he pounces upon his prey; the rattlesnake gives his deadly rattle before he vomits his venom in the veins of his victim; the adder gives his deadly hiss before fastening his fangs in the flesh of his prey; but liquor blights the mind, kills the body and murders the soul without a warning sound.

One sin begets another, and there is a growth in sin just as surely as there is in righteousness. They were easily led by liquor to profanity. Belshazzar commanded, " to bring the golden and silver vessels which his father, Nebuchadnezzar, had taken out of the temple which was in Jerusalem, and the King, and his lords, his wives and his concubines, drank in them."

Think of the unspeakable profanation of using the communion set for bacchanalian revelry! The species of profanation to which we as a nation are most addicted is that of taking the name of God in vain. Swearing has become so common that one may take the name of the Lord in vain and yet be esteemed a gentleman. The father who curses is not fit to associate with his own children. He makes of his mouth a sewer for the filth of his sin-saturated soul. It requires neither brains nor bravery to swear. The inmate of a mad-house may be noted for his profanity. Why not take in vain the name of the dead mother? Surely she was no better friend than Jesus who died that we might live. This sin defiles the sacred memories of youth and does despite to the cradle and the grave.

Some years ago a young man was dying of delirium tremens in Fort Wrangel, Alaska. In his delirium he gave vent to the most horrible oaths. Yet the memories of his childhood were with him in his dying hour. One moment he would utter a dreadful oath, and scarcely would the echo of his oath die away before he would say, " Now I lay me down to sleep." Again a terrible oath, and then, " If I should die before I wake, I pray the Lord my soul to take." The Kingdom of Light and Darkness fighting amid the shadows for an immortal soul!

The second stage of the banquet was one of gloom. Comedy rapidly changes to tragedy, deep and dark.   We are told that " in the same hour came forth the fingers of a man's hand." Mark you, the " same hour." Will not the Lord let the drunken wretches have an hour to themselves? The sparkling champagne; the wild excitement of the gaming table; the voluptuous whirl of the ballroom; a fiery flash of pleasure, and then—hell. The King's " knees smote one against another." His defiant attitude has vanished, his boasted courage gone, and he stands the cringing coward before Him with whom he must reckon. An artist of more than ordinary merit tried to place on canvas this tragic scene. When he came to depict the horror on the face of Belshazzar he could paint nothing that would satisfy his conception of the terrible despair that clouded the King's countenance. The picture may yet be seen, but is still unfinished. The King sent quickly for the astrologers to interpret the writing on the wall. They confessed themselves unable to read the writing. The children of the Devil cannot read God's handwriting. Only the child of Christ can decipher the chirography of Christ. It is significant

that he did not ask the companions of his
drunken debauch to come to his rescue.   The
dying man never sends for his associates in sin
to help him die.   The young lady never asks
for her ballroom companions to console her
dying hour.   At last he has recourse to the
servant of the God he had defied.   Rest assured the good man will have his day.   It may
not be till the death-damp gathers on the brow,
but his day will come.

The third stage of this banquet was the
grave.   Gaiety, gloom and the grave are the
three acts in the drama of the downward life.
We cannot bar God and death from the banquet hall.   Though the city was besieged, the
King and his company felt perfectly safe.   Let
us never forget that there is no safety in sin.
An avenging Nemesis follows fast, and faster,
on the path of the wicked.   The night was
never too dark, or the wind too cold, for God
to find and destroy the citadel of sin.   While
song and dance, drunkenness and lust were at
their height the besieging army divert the
waters of the Euphrates, enter the city and
batter down the doors of the banquet hall.
And now, die, Belshazzar, die!   He has lived
the life of a demon, let him die the death of a

dog! His royal robes are rolled in blood. From a banquet hall to hell!

If our eyes were permitted to see it, we might even now behold the handwriting of the fate of some who are here to-night. The fact that you have been spared to see this hour is due to the mercy of God. Christ loves you, and yearns to see you saved. The wife of a poor drunkard sought my advice as to the wisdom of leaving her husband. She stated that her life and the lives of her children were in danger. I told her that under the circumstances I did not believe that God required her to live with him. On the following day I visited the home. While urging him to quit his drinking and be a real man and a true Christian his little daughter of six or seven years of age walked into the room. Surprised at seeing her, I said: "Why, Mary, what are you doing here? I thought you were with your mamma." Quickly came the reply, "Papa needed me, and I couldn't leave my papa, because I love my papa." Jesus loves you and still lingers with you that He may save you. He gave His life for you. Will you not give your life to Him? Come, for all things are ready!

IX

THE FOOL

But God said unto him, Thou fool, this night thy soul shall be required of thee.—LUKE 12 : 20.

THIS man was everything but a fool in the common acceptation of the word. He was wise in the wisdom of this world, and his folly consisted not in a lack of knowledge, but of true wisdom. He doubtless possessed culture, but it was of the Christless variety. He knew things, but he did not know God, and was therefore a stranger to true wisdom.

First of all, his folly consisted in leaving God out of his calculations. In his scheme of life there was no place for God. With infinite selfishness he speaks of "my" fruits and barns. He believed in a gospel of the world. The gospel of this world says eat, drink and be merry. The Gospel of Jesus Christ says lay up for yourselves treasures where neither moth nor rust doth corrupt, nor thieves break through and steal. The gospel of this world glorifies man; the Gospel of Jesus Christ glorifies God. Quite positively He says, " I " will build greater barns. " I " died on Calvary where Christ died for others. It should no longer be " me and mine," but " you and yours." He lived for what he could to get out of the world rather than what he could put into it. Doubtless he was what his contemporaries termed a " fine business man." Obviously, he had succeeded in business. He made, according to the generally accepted rule, a great success of life; yet in the sight of God, his life was an inglorious failure. Some will have to correct their estimate of success and failure. The failure of success and the success of failure might prove a profitable study.

It is reasonable to suppose he was a very busy man; too busy, indeed, to think of going to church, though he may have had an opportunity of attending the great revival conducted by John the Baptist. He had no time for the Gospel, but he took time for the grave. With all his shrewdness, he didn't have sense enough to keep the Devil from cheating him out of his soul. Surely a man is a fool who, in spite of redeeming love, will spend eternity in perdition.

His folly was evidenced by his thinking

that his body was worth more than his soul. His entire thought seemed to be concerning his body rather than his soul. He planned and toiled that his material desires might be gratified, while his soul was starving for the bread of life. Many spend more time looking in the mirror than in the Bible. A large portion of this congregation consulted the mirror this evening before starting to the house of God; yet how few, perhaps, consulted Christ. Not a few mothers make of their daughters a mere clothes-line to hang something on. The body may be clothed in satin, or broadcloth, and yet the soul sink in hell. The only man that ever reported from perdition was clothed in fine linen and fared sumptuously every day—

" A form more fair or a step more true,
 Ne'er from the heath flower dashed the dew."

The body, however adorned, will furnish a carnival for the earthen worms, yet Christ shed His precious blood that poor, foolish creatures might be wise unto salvation. The story is told of a husband and wife who, over some trivial matter, separated. She left the house and told him to pack her personal apparel in her trunk and send it to her father's home. The following day she received the trunk, and in unpacking it, saw a little pair of red shoes that belonged to her little dead baby. She went to the 'phone and called up her husband and requested him to come and see her. When he came he was ushered into the parlour. On a table, behind which the wife sat, were the red shoes that the dead baby used to wear. She arose to meet him and their eyes rested upon the shoes once worn by the little boy they loved so well. Their love and vows were renewed, and together they returned to the home where baby used to be. Even so, the red blood of the Son of God for sinners slain should reconcile us to God. His folly was further evidenced by his believing riches would bring contentment to the soul. " Hear Him, soul, take thine ease, thou hast much goods laid up for many years." Material things can never satisfy a spiritual need. An immortal soul cannot be fed on " much goods." A man may be contented with riches, but riches never brought contentment. The soul, as well as the body, must be satisfied; and only God can bring contentment and joy to an immortal soul. With Christ there may be contentment in an humble hut, and a palace without Him is a prison.

His question, " What shall I do? " prompted by the fact that he had not enough of room to store his abundant crops, was selfishness personified. About him were the widow and orphan and half-clothed men and women. It seems never to have occurred to him that God had blessed him with wealth that he might be a blessing to others. He was the trustee of a sacred trust that he administered for himself, and not his Lord. When Vanderbilt was dying he asked that his gardener be brought to his bedside. He then requested him to sing, " Come ye sinners, poor and needy." Doubtless he had heard him sing this blessed old song as he worked in the garden. We are all at best poor, needy creatures; only Christ can supply our needs.

Riches may bring pleasure, but pleasure does not bring happiness of heart. The very pleasures for which some seem willing to sell their souls, like the apples of Sodom, will turn to ashes on the lips.

" Pleasures are like poppies spread,
  Touch the flower, the bloom is dead;
  Or like the snowflake on the river,
  A moment white then gone forever."

Our people are fast becoming a pleasure-loving people. The Sunday picture show supplants the church, yet how true,

> " This world is all a fleeting show,
>   To man's illusion given ;
>   Deceitful shine, deceitful show,
>   There's nothing true but Heaven."

The folly of sin always ends in disaster. With hardly a moment's warning he was called to meet his God and give an account of the deeds done in the body. While glorifying in his " much goods laid up for many years," God said, " Thou fool, this night thy soul shall be required of thee." He had the goods laid up, but not the years. Time belongs to God, and the bounds of our habitation are fixed by Him. All unconsciously some of us are tonight nearing the day of destiny. Long ago the fiat of fate has fixed the hour of our departure. We can well imagine he pleaded for time, but his plea was in vain. The years that God had given him had been spent in unspeakable folly, and he had no right to ask for further time. He had taken the time that was given him to rob God and murder his own soul, and now the fool must meet his well-deserved fate. God does not request, but " requires " his soul. Owing to his financial stand-

ing, his obsequious neighbours, with undue
deference, " requested " favours, but God demands an accounting.   His " much goods "
did not make his dying bed as soft as downy
pillows are.   He must stand before the Judgment bar of God and give an account of how
he " got and used his gold."   It is sad enough
to lose wealth, or health, or mind, but it is
infinitely sadder to lose the soul.   Well may
we ask, What shall it profit a man if he gain
the whole world and lose his own soul?

Now that he is dead, what has he left to the
world, and what does he carry to God?   We
may be assured that he receives a pretentious
funeral, but let us not envy him a gorgeous
funeral, as it is the last, and all, the world he
served can give him.   Beautiful and expensive
flowers adorn the grave that contains all that is
mortal of a life without hope and without God.
The casket is of cedar, copper-lined and cov-
ered with black broadcloth, but these will not
prevent the body from returning to the dust
from whence it came.   Bury him out of sight, in
a godless grave, wrapped in a Christless shroud,
to awake to a resurrection of eternal punishment!   Perchance in other days, as the passer-
by gazed on his broad acres and beautiful

mansion, he envied him his lot in life. But no one envies him now. His property, with or without a will, has gone to others, and he is a bankrupt for two worlds. Six feet of earth of his many acres is all that is left him. The body that he pampered will soon decay.

The record tells us nothing of his family, though we may be sure that they were influenced by his godless life. In the dismal abode of the damned he might one day say, " Oh, wife, are you here? And Henry and Tom and May—our whole family, we are all in hell together." There may be families here to-night in which there is not a Christian. I can possibly stand as much of suffering as the average man, but may God deliver me from having to meet my family in perdition, and hear the words: " Husband, father, we followed you here." God grant that we may be wise and lay up for ourselves treasures where neither moth nor rust doth corrupt, nor thieves break through and steal.

Christ loves you and died to redeem your poor lost soul. Seek ye the Lord while He may be found, call upon Him while He is near.

Many years ago a man with his bride went West to build a home and a fortune. He built a home in a sparsely settled section of Western Texas. One day he rode some twenty miles away with a sack of corn. As he was about to return the old miller said to him that he had better not attempt to return home, as a norther would come that evening. He persisted in going, and soon was in the midst of a blinding snow-storm. Then came the bitter cold. As best he could he kept on his way. His horse being exhausted, fell by the wayside and soon froze to death. Wearied and worn, he continued his journey on foot. The next morning his lifeless body was found a short distance from his home. All through the long, awful night his wife sat by the window with a lamp, hoping that he might see the light and be guided home. Frozen to death and in sight of home! Perhaps there may be some one here to-night who is in sight of the Heavenly Kingdom and yet may die without the fold. May God help you to be wise, and seek the Lord while He may be found, and call upon Him while He is near!

X

BACKSLIDING

'And he wist not the Lord was departed from him.—JUDGES 16 : 20.

GROWTH is the law of life, and development the order of the hour. Progress is pleasing, and growth gratifying. The growing grass, the blooming flower and the running river command admiration in the process of progress, yet in spite of the manifest mission of life, backsliding is a frequent and melancholy fact. It is sad to see a strong body weakened and wasted, going backward—a case of physical backsliding. Sadder still, to see one who has been gifted with a strong mind become intellectually inert and impotent; in other words, a mental backslider. Saddest of all, to see one who has been useful in the Church and enthusiastic in Christian service, lose interest in spiritual things and drift away from the Church, and lose power with God and man.

The *fact* of backsliding is one that constantly confronts the churches and imperils their power. The two common kinds of backsliding are the conscious and unconscious. Many backsliders are conscious of their backslidden condition. They realize the soulful songs they used to sing are now as tinkling cymbals and sounding brass. The prayers of the sanctuary no longer stir their souls and incite to more unselfish service. The sermon no longer comes as a message from God to move them to more heroic endeavour. Their souls thirst no more for God and His grace. They hear no more God's stately steppings along the "long-drawn aisles"; the Saviour is seen no more in the pew, or the presence and power of the Holy Spirit manifest in all the sanctuary. With infinite sadness of soul they sing:

> "The peaceful hours I once enjoyed,
> How sweet their memory still,
> But they have left an aching void,
> The world can never fill."

Many have backslidden and yet are unconscious of their deplorable plight. Their spiritual sensibilities are blighted, and they cannot discern their backslidden state. While they have no joy in their religion, they console themselves with the delusion that they are as good as others. They are constantly comparing themselves with themselves, and cherish a state of comparative piety. They make a molehill of their own imperfections and a mountain of the imperfections of others. Because of blurred vision, they " see no harm " in hurtful things. Truly we may have eyes and see not. The story is told of the visit of a lady, who had suddenly acquired wealth, to Turner's studio. After looking at an autumn scene, she said: " Mr. Turner, I can't see anything especially good in that picture." " Ah," replied the artist, " but don't you wish you could? " She lacked the taste of the artist, and could not discern its beauty. Backsliders become colour blind, and unconsciously lose the power of spiritual discernment. In things of doubtful propriety they fail to give Christ the benefit of the doubt. Though the backslider may not realize his condition, his family and friends are painfully conscious of his backsliding. His conversation is no longer of Christ and his church; his home no more a sanctuary—

" Then kneeling down, to Heaven's Eternal
        King,
    The saint, the father, and the husband
        prays:
  Hope ' spring exulting on triumphant wing,'
    That thus they all shall meet in future
        days:
  They ever bask in uncreated rays,
    No more to sigh or shed the bitter tear,
  Together hymning their Creator's praise,
    In such society, yet still more dear;
  While circling Time moves round in an
        eternal sphere."

Like poor Sampson, will you discover your
backsliding in unspeakable tragedy. Though
he knew not of his loss of power, yet it was
revealed to him in his own undoing and death.
Yet, even as God had mercy on him, He will
now have mercy on you. Like Sampson, you
may have a saved soul and a lost life.

One of the best evidences of backsliding is
an indisposition and inability to do personal
work. Many wonder why they are unable to
engage in this needed and splendid service.
The usual reason is that of backsliding. Am
I speaking to a parent who cannot take the
child in the room alone and by prayer and entreaty try to lead him to Christ? Such a one
may have good reason for believing he is a
backslider. We cannot excuse ourselves on

the ground that we do not know how to talk
to one about his soul. It is not a flow of
words but of soul we need; not more of understanding, but of consecration. Without doubt,
the arrested progress of the churches is due,
in large measure, to backslidden members.
We are saved to serve, and hence service is the
normal condition of the child of God. Let us
awake to our backsliding and go work in His
vineyard!

Only a few of the current causes of backsliding can be considered. Chiefest among
these, perhaps, is the neglect of secret prayer.
We may prosper spiritually without public
prayer, but no Christian can neglect secret
prayer and not backslide. One of the first and
surest evidences of backsliding is a failure to
enter the closet and pray to thy Father in secret. The soul seeks and finds itself and its
Saviour when it whispers its wants into the
listening ears of the Eternal. In secret prayer
we walk with God amid the eternal solitudes
of the soul and hold fellowship with the Most
High.

Sweet the story of two men who were traveling in search of coal land. They carried a
considerable sum of money with them far

into the mountains. As night came on they approached a little mountain hut and requested the privilege of spending the night. The old mountaineer informed them they would be welcome, but that the unfinished room in the attic was all he had to offer. They promptly accepted his offer and proffered him pay. This he promptly declined. After the scant evening meal they climbed a ladder to their sleeping apartment. Before sleeping, one said to the other, " I don't like the looks of the old man, so you stay awake and watch till midnight, then awaken me, and I will watch the rest of the night." Before either slept, they heard the old man pray:

" Lord, bless our home, and make us faithful and humble in Thy sight. Lord, bless our daughter far away in the West, and our boy at school. And, Lord, remember in much mercy the strangers under our roof. God bless the loved ones they have left behind, and keep us all by Thy grace and power."

In subdued and choking voice, one whispered to the other, " Go to sleep; there's no danger here." There is always peace and safety in the home where prayer is wont to be made.

Another cause of backsliding is the neglect

of church relations. No one can neglect his church and be true to Christ, the great Head of the Church. Whatever the excuse, he who willfully neglects his church is a backslider. He may be safely counted upon to offer some seeming justification, indeed, most any one but the true one—backsliding. As he may suggest, the church may be " cold," and certainly it is colder because of his conduct.

A little thought will convince us that a man falls out with his Christ before he falls out with his church, and loses power with God before he does with God's people. Many, too, on account of backsliding, fail to move their membership.

In seeking a home the matter of church privileges should receive careful consideration. The vain excuses for permitting church membership to remain far from one's place of abode is usually too silly to merit serious consideration. The fact that a loved one is buried in the graveyard hard by the old church is less than no excuse for holding membership in such a church. God's word, and not the geography of a graveyard, should determine the question of church membership. I have never thought much of the match that will only strike on its

own box, and less of the church member whose
membership will not stand transplanting.
Backsliding is the all-sufficient explanation.
When Christ fills the heart unjust criticisms
depart. Were it not for our low state of piety
we would love the Church as the Bride of
Christ.

An unforgiving spirit invariably contributes
to backsliding. Like a cancer, malice grows
at the very vitals of the soul. Even Pilate and
Herod made friends over a crucified Christ,
and surely all Christians can meet in forgiveness at the Cross. The man who cannot forgive may well ask if Christ has forgiven him.
We pray: " Forgive us our trespasses, as we
have forgiven those who trespass against us."
If we have not forgiven those who trespass
against us, do we not pray that God may not
forgive us? We may well take heed how we
pray.

For our own sake; for the sake of others,
and above all, for Christ's sake, we cannot
indulge the sin of backsliding; and we must
backslide if we fail to forgive. Full and free
forgiveness is well illustrated by the wife
whose drunken and brutal husband had beaten
her into insensibility. The inhuman husband

attempted to escape, but was brought to her bed that she might identify him, so he could be convicted of his crime. Becoming conscious a few moments before her death, she was asked by an officer if her husband, who stood beside the bed, was the man who had so cruelly beaten her. She knew full well that it was he, but with a forgiveness that knew no bounds, she motioned him to her side and, planting a kiss of deathless devotion on his accursed cheek, she answered, " No, he is not the man."

The same God from whom we backslide is the same God who says, " I will heal all your backsliding." The door is open, and God stands ready to welcome the wanderer home. You will find the old home just where you left it. Yet the home did not go to the Prodigal, but the Prodigal returned to the home. Oh, that you should return to the old home to-night, and it will seem all the dearer for your absence. Even our backslidings may be transformed into blessings. It may be that Peter could have never written his glorious epistles had he not denied his Lord. God forbid we should sin because grace abounds; yet God forbid we should make of none effect His grace because sin abounds.

44262

The heavy train unable to mount the grade gains power by going back that enables it to speed on its way. The zigzag lightning darts up and down, but all the while gains power to smite the mighty oak. Humbled by your backsliding, return unto the Lord, who will have mercy upon you, and unto our God who will abundantly pardon—

> "Return, oh Holy Dove! return,
>   Sweet messenger of rest!
> I hate the sins that made Thee mourn,
>   And drove Thee from my breast."

May your prayer be that the Lord will restore unto you the joys of His salvation, that you may teach transgressors the way, and that sinners may be turned unto righteousness. When thou art converted strengthen the brethren. Many about you await the word you will never speak until God has healed your backslidings. It may be your backsliding has thus far barred the door of hope to some lost soul. Hear Him! "Behold I stand at the door and knock. If any man will hear my voice and open the door, I will come in and sup with him, and he with me." He is knocking to-night; let Him in, lest He return no more. Let the Saviour in!

XI

REPENTANCE

Except ye repent, ye shall all likewise perish.—LUKE 13:3.

THE doctrine of repentance is, perhaps, the most neglected of all the great doctrines of the Bible. It is a sad fact that repentance no longer has a place in much of the preaching of to-day. This indispensable doctrine has not only been discredited in the house of its supposed friends but discarded alike by friend and foe as no longer necessary to the forgiveness of sin. This, too, in spite of the fact that there never has been and never can be a really great revival, unless repentance has had its proper place in preaching. It is quite safe to say that we cannot reasonably have a genuine and widespread revival until there is a revival of preaching the doctrine of repentance. It is still true, and will remain true till God's word is changed, that "unless ye repent ye shall all likewise perish."

To such an extent has this essential to salvation been ignored that in many quarters its meaning has been obscured and definition is as much needed as emphasis. Let us then inquire—what is repentance? Negatively, it is not simply sorrow. Many a criminal has exercised great sorrow, not over the awful guilt of sin but because his sin has been exposed. It is the disgrace and the legal penalty rather than sorrow for his sin that starts his tears. The drunkard may shed tears over the fact of his drunkenness and apparently repent, yet continue in his drunkenness. Neither is it, as often defined, a mere " turning around."

Some time since we heard an evangelist give this illustration of repentance: "A man boarded a train to go to a certain place. He soon discovered he was on the wrong train, so he got off the train he was on and took one going in the opposite direction." It should be unnecessary to say that the man who commits his life to this theory of repentance will inevitably be lost. Let us beware lest we accept a counterfeit for the true coin. God abominates feigned repentance.

"Alms with a trumpet, a fast with a sour face, devotion that devoureth widows' houses do more provoke Him to wrath than those vices which these outward formalities seem to cry down. Nothing is so distasteful to Him as a compounded Christian, made up of a bended knee and a stiff neck." Real repentance consists first of all in the perception that one is a lost sinner, without hope and without God. His soul is convicted of sin and he realizes that he has sinned against God and broken His righteous law. Such a realization is attended by a godly sorrow, not to be repented of. This sorrow causes him to hate sin and turn from sin to the Saviour for mercy and deliverance. Dr. Fuller says, " To repent is to accuse and condemn ourselves, to charge upon ourselves the desert of hell, to take part with God against ourselves and to justify Him in all He does against us; to be ashamed and confounded for our sins."

It would probably be difficult to find a better definition of repentance than that given in the Shorter Catechism: " Repentance unto life is a saving grace whereby a sinner out of a true sense of his sin and an apprehension of the mercy of God in Christ doth with grief and hatred of his sin turn from it unto God with full purpose of and endeavour after new obedience." It is well to note the necessity of a true sense of sin being associated with the apprehension of mercy. It has been well said that the former by itself would engender despair, would "work death." The latter, without the former, could it subsist, would inspire presumption. It is the union of the two that produces true repentance, repentance unto life. Archbishop Trench says: "Repentance, literally, is after-knowledge, and then it signifies the change of mind consequent on this after-knowledge; and next, regret for the course pursued, resulting from the change of mind consequent on this after-knowledge; and last of all, change of conduct springing from all this." Heaven knows there has been enough of sin in our lives to break our hearts and bring us home. In spite of numberless sins, God's signal mercy has been displayed in our lives, and God grant this mercy shall not be in vain.

To put it concisely, repentance is a conviction of sin that produces sorrow, and sufficient sorrow to cause us to renounce sin and accept Jesus Christ. When the heart has been "pierced," we are ready to cry, "Men and brethren, what must we do to be saved?"

Over the bed of Augustine were these words: "The sacrifices of God are a broken and contrite spirit." No man's life will be mended till his heart is broken. The heart that is truly penitent will be broken on account of sin and from sin.

Repentance is not so much a prolonged process as an instantaneous act. And just here it is well to note that there is a very vast difference between penance and repentance. Penance is purely a human act, while repentance is a state produced by the Holy Spirit. In penance the individual offers his own suffering as a ground for forgiveness, while in repentance the cause is the shed blood of Christ. The one is based on human merit, the other Divine merit. Some one has said that we were all "dead in trespasses and sins," and must have forever lain both under the punishment and guilt of our transgressions, had not the blessed Jesus opened to us the gates of heaven and sealed a Gospel of repentance with His own blood for the remission of our sins.

God, and not man, is the source of repentance. It is not the work of man but the gift of God, who gives repentance, as well as pardon. Repentance is as much a work of grace as forgiveness of sins. A broken and contrite heart, and a cleansed soul, is the result of sanctifying grace and comes from Him from whom all blessings flow. It is a gracious gift of God and the direct result of the operation of the Holy Spirit. It is the province of the Holy Spirit to convince of sin and the judgment to come. Repentance cannot be produced by sentiment or remorse. The heart of stone may be shattered and its fragments will still be stone. Outward sin may be forsaken from motives foreign to the spirit of true repentance. For moral or financial reasons he may lay aside many of his sins. Epictetus has wisely said that to be good we must first believe we are bad, or as Martensen puts it, " In true repentance the honest will, to be redeemed, asserts itself and the man submits to be redeemed, to be justified before God, and that of pure grace. Since repentance is not the work of man he cannot repent when he wills but when God wills. There is no greater fallacy than that man can repent at his leisure or pleasure. He can find no place for repentance until God makes the place and brings the power. It is, however, our duty and privilege to accept repentance when God offers it. He who continually refuses to repent may, one day, find it impossible to repent. " See to it that repentance come not upon you at that time when the only thing that remains for you is despair. He that hath promised pardon on our repentance hath not promised till we repent. If we put off repentance another day we have a day more to repent of and a day less to repent in."

God's Spirit will not always strive with man. The gift of repentance, though freely offered, may be, and often is, as freely rejected. Every one has a last opportunity to repent, and this last opportunity may come long before life ends. I have listened with intense interest to the auctioneer as he cried, " First; second; third and last chance—sold! " It may be, God only knows, that you have heard and rejected the last call.

One of the surest evidences of genuine repentance is an abhorrence of sin. No one can repent of sin and continue to love sin. He will have an abiding aversion to sin and a righteous indignation against all evil. He will hate sin for its own sake, for his own sake and for Christ's sake. The truly penitent soul shrinks from sin as he would from the bite of the deadly serpent. He has suffered from its poison and will hate sin as he hates Satan the author of sin. He may and will sin, but sin shall not have dominion over him. Counterfeit repentance is like the sailor who throws his goods overboard in a storm and wishes for them when calm comes. It has been said that the repentance of a sinner not convicted of sin is like a blind man running from the flames of a burning house; he runs, he knows not where, and is most likely to stumble in the darkness. The war between the soul and sin will not cease and will be as the war between Rehoboam and Jeroboam—" there was war between Rehoboam and Jeroboam all their days." And just here it may be said that a lack of hatred for sin is one of the deplorable weaknesses of our times. Some have magnified love until they would have us believe that hatred is never justifiable. God Himself hates sin and surely His children should hate it. The man who loves right must hate wrong. A great revival of a holy hatred of sin is deeply to be desired.

The repentant man will not content himself with a hatred of sin, but will turn to righteousness and do good. As has been said, repentance that begins in the humiliation of the heart will end in the reformation of the life. Reformation is the natural sequence of repentance and regeneration. Life can never be the same to one who has seen himself a sinner and turned with sorrow from his sins. Out of his sorrow will come a peace that passes all understanding. Out of the storm the rainbow will be born, and this rainbow will circle with blessing his whole life. The smile of joy will take the place of the tear and gladness will take the place of sorrow. The soul may sorrow for a night, but joy cometh in the morning. Only the eye that has been washed with the penitent tear will behold the King in His beauty.

In these latter times false prophets are telling us that children come into the world in a sinless state, and that with proper environment they would have no need of repentance and regeneration. The gospel of Social Service, as preached by not a few, has served to popularize this soul-destroying doctrine. But what saith the Scriptures: " Unless ye repent, ye shall all likewise perish."

If there be any righteous apart from Christ it is clear that they have no part in the atonement. Christ came not to call the righteous but sinners to repentance. Christ, therefore, is of non-effect to the sinless soul. Only the sinner needs repentance, and only the repentant can share in the glories of the Lord. Salvation by eugenics is not only a poor but an exceedingly sinful substitute for salvation by the blood of Christ. God has commanded all men everywhere to repent, and unless ye repent ye shall " all likewise perish."

God demands that we repent now. To-morrow may be too late. We cannot repent too soon, for we know not how soon it may be too late. Thales, one of the Grecian sages, being urged by his mother to change his condition in life, replied that it was too soon, and later, being again urged, said it was too late. Repentance deferred may mean repentance forever impossible. Esau found no place for repentance, though he sought it diligently, and with tears. His birthright was gone and gone forever. 'Tis said that " of all sad words of tongue or pen the saddest are these, it might have been," but sadder still, " It will never be again." There may be those in this congregation who have already passed the period of repentance. Certainly every day repentance is delayed increases the probability that we will go to death and judgment unforgiven; without God and without hope for all eternity. It has been said that "morning" is the devil's verb; he bids tarry, time enough to repent, but "morning" is God's adverb, and He bids us repent in the morning of youth. His spirit will not always strive with man. There are mighty moments of destiny which settle forever the issues of life and death.

XII

PAST FEELING

Who being past feeling have given themselves over unto lasciviousness, to work all uncleanness with greediness.—EPHESIANS 4: 19.

LIFE has been defined as a series of sensations. However imperfect the definition, the fact remains that where there is no life there is no sensation. This is equally true in the religious realm. The spiritually dead can never experience anything of religious feeling, having passed the point of all feeling. Without doubt,

> " There is a time, we know not when,
> A place, we know not where,
> Which marks the destiny of man
> To glory, or despair."

The condition, though similar in result, should not be confused with the unpardonable sin. The unpardonable sin was a specific act and was committed against the Holy Ghost. There is serious doubt with many that this specific sin can now be committed.   There can, however, be no doubt that one can sin away a day of grace and become insensible to sin. The soul may lose its sensitiveness and the deep shadows of death hover over the pathway of the impenitent.   The condition of the person who enters this state is indeed pitiable. Total spiritual paralysis has settled forever over his soul.   He is beyond the pale of preaching and beyond the power of prayer.   Ephraim is joined to his idols, let him alone.   Why preach to him?   Why pray for him?   Let him alone!   He has said " Good-bye " to God. He has bid adieu to the Holy Spirit.   He has breathed a last farewell to the Saviour, who died to make possible his redemption.   Like the ox, he walks unheeding to his doom.

Naturally we weep over the dead body of a loved one; and yet we sorrow not, as those who have no hope.   There is infinitely greater cause to weep over a dead soul!   Many have reached this state unconscious of their condition.   But few, perhaps, realize when they take the step that can never be retraced.   They may often imagine that some day they will return to the Lord and make secure their salvation. Alas how true,

" There is by us a line unseen,
  That crosses every path;
  The hidden boundary between
  God's patience and His wrath."

Unspeakably sad the fact that one more rejection of offered mercy may place us beyond the bounds of mercy. One more chance for Christ may be the last chance for Christ. My spirit shall not always strive with man, saith the Lord. He that hardeneth his heart and stiffeneth his neck shall be lost, and that, too, without remedy. And yet the Son of God protests against the suicide of the soul. Hear Him! " These hands were pierced for you, why will you crimson your hands in the blood of your own soul? This side was torn by the cruel spear, that there might be opened a fountain in the House of David for sin and uncleanness. These hands were nailed to the Cross that they might be extended in mercy to you."

The story is told of a man who being warned by his faithful watchdog of the approach of the burglar drove the dog back to his kennel. He had hardly fallen asleep until he was awakened by the violent barking of the faithful dog. Angered that his rest was disturbed, he kills the dog and again seeks his rest. While sleeping the burglar robs his home. Alas, many have despised the repeated warnings and done violence to the watchman of their souls. Oh, that we knew the day of our visitation!

A continued rejection of Christ may lead to the point where feeling flees forever from the soul. It is easy for one to lapse into a condition of chronic indecision. Hesitating and halting are often as effective as willful rejection. Really, a failure to decide for Christ is, in its last analysis, a decision against the claims of Christ. But few, perhaps, have willfully decided never to seek Christ. Most men in Christian lands expect some time to seek and find the Saviour. Just what time they know not, and their only concern seems to be that it shall come while they are yet in the land of the living. In speaking to a man concerning his soul, he said: " I some day expect to accept the Saviour." I pressed him to name the day, which he refused to do. I requested him to sign a statement that, God willing, he would give his soul to the Lord's keeping within five years. This he declined to do, with the statement that he might wish to become a Christian long before that time. I then urged him to agree to become a Christian in one year, or one month, or one week. He positively refused to fix any particular date. He failed to take into account the fact that he might sin away a day of grace. His real purpose was to enjoy the pleasures of sin till death stared him in the face and then turn to the long neglected Lord as the last resort. The body may live long after the soul is dead. The old, old saying—"As long as there is life there is hope," is not only dangerous, but wholly untrue. There is life without hope, and without God for this world and the world to come.

You have everything before you that you can ever hope to have to aid you settling the destiny of your soul. The crucified Christ is uplifted before you; the Holy Spirit seeks to do His perfect work in your sinful soul and God's men and women are entreating a Throne of Grace in your behalf. What more can you wish or hope for? You may soon be past feeling and irrevocably committed to the course that leads to perdition. This, too, in spite of the fact that your path to perdition has been blocked by the prayers and made slippery with tears of your loved ones. Continue on the road to ruin and sooner or later you will become the victim of your sins. The eagle that seizes the rattlesnake in its claws and flies far upward in the blue of the skies may imagine he has conquered. But look! the "sky-king" seems fettered in his flight. His wings are weary and he is battling hard to continue his aerial journey. Now, like a leaden ball, downward he dashes, dead, to the earth; while exulting in his apparent victory over his prey his own body was being filled with deadly poison. Sin indulged at last spells death to the body and death to the soul. It may be God's last call, and therefore your last chance.

"Be swift my soul to answer Him,
Be jubilant my feet."

By resisting the Holy Spirit, every heavenly aspiration may die still born in the soul. "My Spirit shall not always strive with man, saith the Lord." While He pleads, reject Him not. Even now you may find it more difficult to turn a deaf ear to His pleadings than to hear and heed His loving entreaty. "To-day, if ye will hear His voice, harden not your heart."

On the night of the Chicago fire Mr. Moody preached to a mighty throng of people and Mr. Sankey closed the service with the song:

" To-day the Saviour calls
    For refuge fly,
    The storm of vengeance falls
    And death is nigh."

Many who heard the sermon and song were consumed by the flames before the dawn of another day. You cannot afford to risk your immortal soul. Oh, my poor lost and deluded friend, I plead with you for your soul's sake, for Christ's sake, don't take the risk.

Christ stands to-night knocking at the door of every unrepentant soul. Let Him in! Let Him in! Should you refuse to open the door, He may turn away, to visit your soul no more forever. Is there yet in your heart any sense of your lost condition? Do you feel the need of a Saviour? In your inmost soul, is there a longing for Him who gave His life that you might have eternal life? If such be true, you are not past feeling; there is yet hope that you may escape hell and gain heaven. The Gates of Mercy are still open, but they will not forever remain ajar. Enter while you may.

" Depths of mercy can there be,
    Mercy still reserved for me."

Before your will is paralyzed and an everlasting numbness settles over your soul; before you are "past feeling," accept the pardon by Grace bestowed. It is only a step to Jesus; why not take it now?

XIII

FAITH

Go thy way, thy faith hath saved thee.—LUKE 7 : 50.

WITHOUT faith it is impossible to please God, and it is the one indispensable condition alike to salvation and service. The Christian life is cradled in faith and must continue with faith till life's latest breath. Surely faith is the substance of things hoped for, the evidence of things not seen. In view, then, of its infinite importance we may well ask—What is faith? This question is the more necessary in view of the fact that even faith has been counterfeited. Faith is not, as sometimes asserted, merely the intellectual assent to a given proposition. I firmly believe that George Washington was the first President of the United States, but the belief in this fact does not demand faith upon my part. Devils, we are told, believe and tremble, but certainly no one would claim that they had faith. The distinction between faith and belief is both real and vital. It is true, they are derived from the same word, but this in no wise makes them similar in meaning. The difficulty comes from the fact that we have no verb form of faith. It would not be deemed proper to say, " I faith it will rain." Hence in choosing a word to express the verb form of faith we are forced to select the word " believe." It is worthy of note that nowhere in the Scriptures is it affirmed we are saved through belief, but it is uniformly declared that we are saved through faith. When the noun is used it is invariably " faith " and not " belief." Faith involves all that belief does, and infinitely more. Faith implies a trust in and a dependence upon. Millions believe that Jesus Christ is the Son of God who are admittedly destitute of faith in Christ. We believe in a thing, but we have faith in a person. The child has faith in its mother, and the same character of faith exercised in Christ would bring salvation.

Faith in Christ carries with it a committing of the life to Christ and a trust in Him as our only hope of salvation. It is highly important that all who are engaged in the work of soul-winning should not only grasp the full meaning of faith but plainly declare the nature and demands of faith upon the lost. A mistake concerning the meaning of faith may cost the life of the soul.

Archdeacon Farrar says that faith in the full range of its Pauline meaning is both a single act and a progressive principle. As a single act it is the self-surrender of the soul to God, the laying hold of Christ, the sole means whereby we appropriate this reconciling love. As a progressive principle, it is the renewal of the personal life in sanctification—a preservation of the " righteousness of God " objectively bestowed upon us in the inward and ever deepening righteousness of our own life, lived in the faith of the Son of God, who loved us and gave Himself for us. Bushnell affirms, with truth, that Christian faith is the faith of a transaction. It is not the committing of one's thought in assent to any proposition, but the trusting of one's being to a Being, there to be rested, kept, guided, moulded, governed and possessed forever. Dr. Cuyler illustrates faith by a miner and a rope. When a miner looks at a rope that is to lower him into the deep mine he may coolly say, " I have faith in that rope as well made and strong," but when he lays hold of it and swings down by it into

the tremendous chasm then he is believing *on*
the rope. Then he is trusting himself to the
rope. It is not a mere opinion, it is an act.
The miner lets go of everything else and bears
his whole weight on those well braided strands
of hemp. "Faith is letting down our nets
into the transparent deeps at the Divine command." It enables the soul, like a ship, to
ride safely at anchor amid the storms of life.

It is not our business to try and analyze the
processes of faith. We can no more master
the mechanism of faith than we can the
processes of redemption. The fact of faith is
sufficient without an attempted chemical
analysis. We might as well conclude to take
out the heart to see if it is working normally
as to be continually dissecting our faith. Faith
looks upward to Christ and not inward to its
own imperfections. The fact and acts of
faith are worth infinitely more than a knowledge of its processes. I was blind but now I
see was sufficient for the man who had received
his sight.

" Faith builds a bridge across the gulf of death,
    To break the shock, blind nature cannot shun,
    And lands thought smoothly on the further
        shore."

There is also a real difference between "faith" and "the faith." Faith, as commonly understood, is used in a subjective sense, and has reference to the faith that insures the salvation of the individual. This may be properly termed saving faith. This is the general use of the word in the Scriptures. There is, however, another well defined use of the term, and this is distinctly objective. In Jude 3 we are commanded to earnestly contend for "the faith" once for all delivered to the saints. Here the word is clearly used in the objective sense. "The faith" is used in this connection to denote the system of New Testament doctrines. Hence it is that one may have saving faith and not be in "the faith." This is seen in the fact that many saved people have a very poor conception of the great doctrines of the Bible. Having received faith, we should strive to know "the faith."

Were it not for our sinful nature, faith in God would be natural to every life. Faith, which was Adam's birthright, was forfeited in Eden. Even now faith is easy to the regenerate soul. We sometimes hear one say, "I'll try and trust him." It does not require any effort for the regenerate soul to trust the Redeemer of that soul. The fact that we are "trying" to trust Christ is evidence of the fact that we are not trusting Him. There is every reason for a saved man to trust his Saviour, and not one why he should distrust Him. This, however, is not true of the unregenerate. It is entirely natural for the lost soul not to trust Christ. This being true, we may well ask, How can we reasonably hope for the lost to be saved? There can be but one answer— Faith is the gift of God. We cannot reason ourselves into faith, but look to Him who is the giver of every good and perfect gift. We may and should sorrow over our sins, but we cannot sorrow ourselves into faith. Unless God gives faith to the soul it must and will remain faithless.

Faith may be illustrated by the little girl who, standing by the trap-door, hears her father calling out of the darkness in the cellar. He urges her to jump and that he will catch her in his arms. She cannot see her father, but her faith triumphs and she leaps in the dark and falls in her father's arms. Faith in God is a leap into everlasting light and love and joy and peace.

Faith saves us in the sense that we cannot be saved without it. It is the conduit that conveys to the sinful soul the cleansing power of the blood of Christ. It may also be likened to the coupling pin that connects the cars to the engine that furnishes the power. There is one, and only one, who can save—the blood of Jesus Christ His Son cleanses us from all sin. Faith makes available the power of His blessed blood that redeems us from the power and penalty of sin. Truly may we sing and pray:

> " Oh, for a faith that will not shrink,
> Though pressed by every foe ;
> That will not falter on the brink,
> Of any earthly woe ;

> " That will not murmur nor complain,
> Beneath the chastening rod,
> But in the hour of grief and pain,
> Will lean upon its God."

We sometimes speak of a " blind faith." As a matter of fact all faith is blind, for we no longer hope for that which we see. In the language of this world, " seeing is believing," but the child of God believes and sees through the eyes of faith. The old story of Casabianca, who was told by his father to stand at a certain place on the ship till he returned, beautifully illustrates the child's faith in his father. Though the flames were nearing him, he stood unmoved, calmly awaiting death or his father's return.

> " Yet beautiful and bright he stood,
> As though born to rule the storm
> A creature of heroic mould,
> Was that proud, but child-like form."

It is important that we bear in mind there are degrees in faith. One may have faith as a mustard seed, but if it is true faith he shall yet see God reconciled. The disciples asked that the Lord would " increase " their faith. Christ said concerning the Centurion, " I have not found so great faith, no not in all Israel." Faith should be a constant growth from the moment we trust Him till we shall see Him face to face and be satisfied. It is true that many do not possess the full assurance of faith, though this is possible and should be the portion of every believer. With Job we should be able to say, " I know that my Redeemer liveth." And with Paul, " I know Him whom I have believed." Yet one should not refuse to confess his faith in Christ because he does not possess the full assurance of faith. It may be that you are one of " little faith," yet blessed are you if you have faith. To be satisfied with " little faith " is unfortunate, but to despise it is more than foolish. Honest doubt may lay the foundations for an unshaken faith.

We should be careful to distinguish between faith and feeling. We are not saved by feeling, or faith and feeling. Our feelings cannot be substituted for faith. One's feelings can never become the medium of forgiveness. Feelings, at best, are the result and not the procuring cause of our salvation. A man should pay his debts, whether he feels like it or not. No amount of feeling can excuse us from doing our duty. God so loved the world that He gave His only begotten Son that whosoever " believeth " in Him should not perish but have everlasting life. Many, alas, are deterred from confessing their faith in Christ because they do not feel as they imagine one should who is saved. In other words, they have allowed their feelings, or rather their lack of feelings, to function instead of faith. Feelings have their moods and tenses, but the fundamentals of saving faith are essentially and forever the same. Faith may have its clouds, but it makes of them but a background for the many-coloured rainbow. Feelings are accidental and circumstantial, but faith sustains us in life and is a bridge on which we cross the River of Death, leaning on the everlasting arms. " Faith converses with the angels, and antedates the hymns of glory; every man that hath this grace is as certain that there are glories for him as if he had heard and sung the thanksgiving song for the blessed sentence of doomsday."

It goes without saying that a false faith, however honest and fervent, will not bring salvation. Many appear to believe that all that is necessary is for one to have faith. How frequently do we hear, " If I am honest in my faith, I am all right." Better a man be dishonest in a false faith than to be honest in it. If honest in an untrue faith, the probability is that he will continue in it to the end. The fact that one takes strychnine, honestly believing it to be quinine, does not make the strychnine harmless. The glory of faith is in its object rather than in its exercise. The mere intensity of faith cannot determine its character. A false faith is as powerless as a false god. The curse of our times is not so much a lack of faith as the lack of the true faith.

Many stagger at the plan of salvation by

grace through faith, yet they must practice a kind of faith every day that they live. Faith is the basis not only of the religious but of social, financial and political life. Strike it from the history of the world and there is but little left. Let the people lose faith in a bank and its doors must close. The man who accepts a check in payment of an account evidences his faith in the maker of the check. The entire fabric of the business world is built on faith. A bankrupt home is the result of a loss of faith on the part of husband or wife. Without faith there would be no marriage and all social life would collapse. Even science, which some have supposed to be contrary to faith, has its genesis in faith. The first principles of science are assumed. Uniformity is an essential assumption of science. Many things in this life we must believe on the evidence of others, and not by our own personal knowledge.

When a judge was about to pass sentence on a criminal convicted of murder he asked if the prisoner had anything to say why sentence should not be passed upon him. The prisoner's son said, " Yes, Mr. Judge, I want to say papa did not kill that man." The kindly judge said, " My boy, your father has been convicted by twelve men, and why do you say he is not guilty? " The little fellow replied, " My papa told me he didn't kill him, and my papa never told me a story."

> " Ere since by faith I saw the stream,
>   Thy flowing wounds supply;
>   Redeeming love has been my theme,
>   And shall be till I die."

XIV

A PILGRIMAGE

We are journeying unto the place of which Jehovah said, I will give it to you: come thou with us, and we will do thee good; for Jehovah hath spoken good concerning Israel.
—NUMBERS 10: 29.

LIFE in this world is a pilgrimage from the cradle to the grave. Here we have no continuing city, but we hope for, if we do not seek one, in the world to come. Across the barren wastes of time there are many pathways, but they all lead to one goal— the grave. Over hill and plain together we go and then " down the valley one by one." Though brief our earthly pilgrimage, it determines our eternal destiny. At this moment we are, one and all, traveling the road that leads to eternal life or everlasting destruction. While crossing the Atlantic a ship passed us within hailing distance. The captain of the ship cried across the stormy waters, " Whither bound? " Back went the reply, " Liverpool." To-night I would ask of every soul in this presence, " Whither bound? "

Our text is an invitation given by Moses to his father-in-law to accompany the Children of Israel to the Holy Land. Moses was, as we should be, deeply interested in those of his household. Sweet the thought of all the family, without the loss of one, reunited in the Kingdom of the Unsetting Sun. No more gracious or blessed invitation could have come to this man who was a stranger to Israel's God. It was a great opportunity for service. What a mighty service he could have rendered the friends of God. Acquainted as he was with the trackless desert he would be, as Moses said, " eyes " for them.

It is true, they greatly needed him, yet he needed them even more. There are probably those here who could be of infinite service to the cause of Christ, but Christ can render infinitely greater service to them. We can serve, but Christ only can save that we may serve. Let us never imagine that God's Kingdom cannot get along without us. Heaven will be none the poorer for the lack of our presence.

The invitation, perchance, seemed a trifle to this man of the desert, yet perfection is made up of trifles and perfection is not a trifle. It is not the extraordinary thing that is needed, but the ordinary thing done in an extraordinary way. After all, every timely invitation is a challenge and every rightful challenge a command. An opportunity for Christ is an obligation to God. We may reject the invitation to service, but we cannot escape the penalty of rejecting the invitation. When Christ invited Matthew to come with Him he did not hesitate but immediately rose up and followed Him. There are but two things to do with the invitations of Christ—accept them or reject them. It is true the invitation involved hardship; yet in the Kingdom of God and man, there is no excellence without sacrifice and suffering. To have the power we must pay the price; to wear the crown we must endure the Cross. I would not have you believe that the Christian life is one of ease and comfort. To the contrary, it is one of toil and tears. I invite you to self-sacrifice and self-immolation. I invite you to lose your life here that you may find it by and by. I invite you to a living death that you may have a deathless life.   In spite of the hardships of the way, it is the only way that leads home.   It is our duty to enlist in His service, at whatever cost. We must choose between the firing line and the fate of the traitor.   When Commodore Dewey's squadron was entering Manila Bay the commander of the ship that was leading the attack signaled, "Torpedoes ahead." From Dewey's flagship back flashed the reply, "Steam ahead."   A moment more and the signal, "Torpedoes are exploding about us." Quick the answer, "Steam ahead."   In spite of screaming shell and bursting torpedo, they steamed ahead to glorious victory!

The journey would prove profitable to Hobab.   In spite of appearances, it pays to be pious, and righteousness shall have its reward. God had promised good to Israel and he would share in the promised blessings.   The reverse side of every invitation extended by Christ is a promise made by Christ.   The question of accepting Christ is one of profit and loss, and what shall it profit a man if he gain the whole world and lose his own soul?   Eternity with Satan, and without the Saviour!   The soul which is lost is lost in spite of all that Christ could do to save that soul.   Omnipotence exhausted itself in the act of Atonement. Hard by the railway there was a little cottage on the hillside. The little girl in the home would wave to the engineer as the train passed. On nearing the home the engineer would blow his whistle and quickly the child would appear, waving a passing welcome. One day he blew his whistle and gazed expectantly at the door of the humble home. Missing his little friend his eyes turned to the track, and not far ahead, in the center of the track, stood the little girl waving her tiny hands. As quick as thought he reverses his engine, applies his brakes, and crawls along the boiler to the pilot. As the train moves slowly to the child he reaches out his hand and snatches her from the track. Overcome by the terrible strain, his heart ceases to beat and he falls dead from the pilot! At the cost of His own life Christ rescues a lost world from impending doom!

Like many a lost sinner, Hobab rejects the invitation to return to his own people. Happy the man who knows his friends and properly appreciates their advice. Not our best friends, yea, not even father or mother, or child, should be permitted to stand between the soul and its duty to God. Evermore it is true that unless we would be willing to forsake father and mother and houses and lands and take up our cross and follow Him, we are not worthy of Him. Shall we not say, " Master, we have left all and followed Thee "? Like Moses, will we not choose affliction with the people of God rather than the pleasures of sin for a season?

Fortunately, Hobab reversed his decision and walked in the path that lead to the glory of God and the good of his own soul. He did accompany the children of Israel and land was set apart in Palestine for his people. There may be a perverse and wicked young man here to-night who has often rejected the Saviour who will one day preach the glorious Gospel of the Son of God. Let us not be discouraged, because some loved one has oft turned a deaf ear to the entreaties of the Gospel. They may yet turn their step towards Zion!

Paul, the persecutor, becomes the prince of preachers. Lips that now speak despitefully of Him may one day sing His praises. The world-famed Gipsy Smith was converted while yet in a gypsy camp. He and his mother were stricken with smallpox. The mother grew steadily worse, while " Gipsy " continued to improve. The father, who was nursing both,

left for a moment the bedside of his wife to
visit the tent where a "gypsy boy lay." Standing by his bedside he said, " Gipsy, your
mother is mighty sick and I don't know
whether she knows about Jesus or not. Do
you feel able to go and speak to her?"
Hardly had he spoken the words when, from
the near-by tent, came the words of the song,
" My Lord calls and I must go to meet Him in
the promised land." The father supporting
the son, silently and slowly they made their
way to the mother's tent. She lifted her eyes,
fast closing upon the scenes of earth. A smile
parted her lips, soon to be set in death. As
they approached her bed she pointed her hand
upward and fell asleep! She was dead! It
was growing dark; night was at hand, but her
soul had winged its way to the realms of endless day and everlasting light!

Oh, come with us and we will do thee good,
for God has promised good to Israel. Come,
before a numbness chills your soul and your
doom forever sealed!

We are one and all rapidly approaching our
journey's end. To many of us it is, perhaps,
much nearer than we have believed. Is there
one here who cannot truthfully sing—

" One sweetly solemn thought,
Comes to me, o'er and o'er;
I am nearer my home to-day
Than I have been before."

Certainly you are nearer death and judgment
than ever before.   The Christ of God and the
Church of God alike bid you come.   Come, for
all things are ready.   He died that you might
live forever! A representative was elected
from one of the districts in Georgia with the
positive understanding he was to vote against
General John B. Gordon for the Senate.   In
an exciting election which soon followed in the
Legislature he cast his vote for General Gordon.   On his return home his constituency,
much displeased, called a mass meeting and
charged him with betraying his trust.   After
several had denounced him for casting his vote
for General Gordon he was given a chance to
defend himself.   He frankly admitted that he
had been elected with the express understanding he was to vote against the man he voted
for.   " I fully intended," he said, " to vote
against General Gordon, but just before casting my vote I happened to look to my right
and my eyes fell upon his kindly face.   On
that face I noted a scar that he received in

fighting our battle. Fellow citizens, when I gazed upon that scar and thought of the courageous and chivalrous record of that man, I could not vote against him." In a moment indignation had turned to tears. The silence was broken by a one-armed veteran, who mounted the platform and moved a vote of thanks to their representative for casting his vote for General John B. Gordon for a seat in the United States Senate. The motion passed without a dissenting vote. Oh, if you could but see the scars of Him whose visage was marred more than the sons of men, you could not reject His claim upon your life and your all.

> " Five bleeding wounds He bears,
>   Received on Calvary."

"And the Spirit and the bride say, Come. And let him that heareth say, Come. And let him that is athirst come. And whosoever will, let him take the water of life freely."

XV

PRAYER

Behold he prayeth.—ACTS 9:11.

IN our great desire for organization and
in magnifying methods, there is danger
lest we forget the privilege and power of
prayer. All of God's blessings are conditioned
on prayer and without faithful fervent prayer
there can be no acceptable service. Perhaps,
as never before, there is a crying need for a revival of the spirit and practice of prayer. A
mighty revival, whether local or world-wide,
is impossible without prayer. If a multitude
of our churches would cease trying to " work
up " a revival and earnestly strive to pray one
down, they would meet with infinitely more
of success. The truth is, many professed
Christians have lost faith in prayer, and hence
in a prayer-hearing and a prayer-answering
God.

Probably no more pertinent question could be propounded than—What is prayer? It is not, as some seem to surmise, an address to the people in the presence of the Lord. All too often we " say our prayers " instead of praying. Paul had been " saying his prayers " for many years, but the first time he really prayed God looked down from His throne on high and said, " Behold he prayeth." Would God He might say the same thing of us, at this moment. Some of us are sadly conscious of the fact that many of our so-called prayers have been but perfunctory performances. There have been many definitions of prayer. One of the simplest and best perhaps is that it is " talking with God." Mr. Spurgeon has said that it is pulling the bell-rope and hearing the bell ring by the throne of God. Martin Luther, with his martial spirit, said that prayer was bombarding the heavens. Another saint has described it as " begging and thanking." This definition would probably be more complete had he said it was praising, thanking and begging. A poet claims that prayer is—

" The soul's sincere desire,
Unuttered or expressed."

" What is prayer? The converse of the soul with God. Faith speaking to God. As our senses put us in connection with visible things so does faith with things unseen; and prayer is the voice of faith. Faith pleading with God. The utterance of strong desire, pleading with prevailing arguments and irresistible warrants."

It is worthy of note that man is the only being that prays. The lower animals are blessed with instinct, but not with the instinct to pray. Yet man prays instinctively, even the unregenerate man. It is natural for the little child to pray and just as natural for the aged man or woman. We may repress the instinct to pray, but when all else fails we turn to prayer. The origin of prayer was probably with Adam and Eve in the Garden of Eden. We know that there were sacrifices in the time of Abel and there could have been no sacrifice without sacrificial prayers. As it has been said, we do not read that men began to " call upon the name of the Lord " until after Seth was born, but we may be quite sure this was not the origin of prayer. There has been no nation where prayer of some kind has not been known. Pythagoras said:

"In all thou dost, first let thy prayers
      ascend,
   And to the gods thy labours first com-
      mend;
   From them implore success, and hope a
      prosperous end."

The Christian finds ample authority for prayer in the fact that Christ commands it and commends it, and is ever ready to listen to the supplications of His children. In the Kensington Museum there is a picture of Dr. Johnson waiting outside in the anteroom of royalty, waiting his turn for an audience. The King of kings never keeps us waiting, but will give us a hearing at any moment. Martin Luther says: "I have so much business to-day that I shall not be able to get through it with less than three hours' prayer." Many of us, under like pressure, would have been disposed to have made the three hours three minutes. If we expect God to guide us we must ask His guidance. The pillar of cloud and fire await us for the asking. In *The Victory Life* there appears the story of Dr. J. J. Lucas, who was for forty-five years a missionary in India. Dr. Lucas says: "The most real thing in my life is the sense and presence of God's guidance." In 1870 he was under appointment to go as mis-

sionary to India.   Word was sent to him and
ten other missionaries who were to accompany
him to be ready to sail October 8th on the
steamship *Cambria*.   Passage had been engaged and all were ready to go.   It was then
urged that they remain over Sunday and be
given a farewell service.   The missionaries
listened to the entreaty and agreed to remain.
The party finally sailed on October 12th.   The
Cambria went down at sea and all were lost
save one, and he, when rescued, was demented.

" Chinese " Gordon used to put a handker-
chief at the opening of his tent when he prayed,
thus saying to the world he must not be disturbed when he was talking to God.   Let the
soul alone in the " closet " whisper its long-
ings into the listening ears of the Eternal.

" The way is dark, my Father! Cloud on cloud
    Is gathering thickly o'er my head, and loud
    The thunders roar above me.   See I stand,
    Like one bewildered!   Father, take my hand,
            And through the gloom
            Lead safely home,
                Thy child."

Well may we ask how should we pray.
First of all, and above all, we should entreat
the Lord to " teach us how to pray."   We may
cultivate the act of praying; but God only can

teach us the science of prayer. There are, however, some things that are absolutely essential to prevailing prayer. Among these faith probably deserves the first place. Whatever else prayer may require, faith is absolutely essential. It is at this point that a multitude of our prayers miscarry. Probably the greatest surprise that could come to some people would be for God to answer their prayers. Many even forget what they pray for. It is hardly reasonable to expect God to remember what we ask for when we ourselves forget it. As faith without works is dead, so is prayer without faith. God will not regard the prayer that is not made in fervent faith. If we would exercise the same faith in our Heavenly Father that the child has in the earthly parent, God would hear and answer our prayers. We should confidently look for and expect an answer to our prayers. Just as one writes a letter and expects an answer, so should we expect a reply to our prayers. The little girl that prayed that God would send her brother and then went home and brought him, demonstrated a real faith in her prayers. It is told of an engineer that a woman asked him what time his train was due at a certain station. He told

her the time the train was due, to which she
replied, " My daughter is dying and that will
be twenty minutes too late." The old engineer
went to the telegraph office and obtained per-
mission to run twenty minutes ahead of time.
Passing the woman on the way to his engine,
he said, " Get aboard; if God will give me ten
minutes, I will make up the other ten minutes."
It is our duty to pray according to our ability
and to get up from our knees and help God
answer our prayers.

We should pray in real earnest. Cold
prayers never warmed a human heart or moved
the heart of God. It is said that one went to
Demosthenes and asked him to plead his cause.
He heard him without attention while he told
his story without earnestness. The man, not-
ing his inattention, cried out, " It is true."
"Ah," said Demosthenes, " I believe you now."
Jacob wrestling with the angel through the
lonely night is a splendid example of earnest
prevailing prayer. Daniel, in spite of the
royal decree, with his windows opened towards
Jerusalem, inspires us to faith in earnest
prayer.

Martin Luther heard that Melancthon was
dying. When he approached the bedside the

symptoms of death were quite apparent.
Melancthon aroused himself and seeing Luther
said: "Oh, Luther, is this you? Why don't
you let me depart in peace?" "We can't
spare you, Philip," was the reply. Luther fell
upon his knees and wrestled with God for more
than an hour for the recovery of his friend.
Again Melancthon said, "Dear Luther, why
don't you let me depart in peace?" The reply
was, "We cannot spare you yet." Luther
then ordered some nourishment, which was refused with the question, "Dear Luther, why
will you not let me go home and be at rest?"
Luther then added, "Take this soup or I will
excommunicate you." He took the soup and
soon regained his wonted strength. When
Luther returned home he said to his wife,
"God gave me my brother Melancthon back
in direct answer to prayer." Who will doubt
but that his life was graciously spared in answer to the prayer of his friend?

> "Oh, how praying rests the weary,
> Prayer can turn the night to day;
> Ere you left your room this morning,
> Did you think to pray?"

XVI

HEAVEN

I go to prepare a place for you.—JOHN 14: 2.

IT is not only the preacher's duty to preach men into heaven, but to preach heaven into men. The Tree of Life blooms on both sides of the River of Time. The man will never taste heaven hereafter who has not had a foretaste of it here. Insurance for eternity should be utilized for time. No man will go to heaven who does not take something of heaven with him. After all, heaven will be more largely determined by what we take there than by what we find there. The man who finds heaven in his home will be sure to find a home in heaven.

In view of the fact that all the followers of Christ hope some day to find the Christian's home in glory, it is little less than amazing that we think and speak so little of the eternal abiding place of the soul. It would seem natural that we should wish to know something of the geography of the country in which we are to spend eternity. In going into a foreign country we rightly consult our guide-book, that we may learn something of its people and places of interest. God has given us a book that will guide us to glory, and tell us, ere we reach it, something of the Glory land. It is our blessed privilege to know something of the character of the place that is being prepared for us by our Lord and Saviour Jesus Christ.

Heaven is preëminently a prepared place for a prepared people. Christ not only prepares the place for a people, but a people for the place. Just as hell is a place prepared by Satan for his children, so is heaven a place prepared for those who have been purchased by the precious blood of Christ. Regeneration is the necessary preparation for the home of the soul. " Except a man be born again, he cannot enter the Kingdom of Heaven."

Heaven has always been conceived of as a place of rest. We live in a world of work and worry, where the cares and toils of time weary the stoutest heart. The task tires, and at times the burden seems more than we can bear. In greater or less degree the life of every man and woman is the Song of the Shirt:

" With fingers weary and worn,
　With eyelids heavy and red,
　A woman sat in unwomanly rags,
　Plying her needle and thread.
　Stitch! Stitch! Stitch!
　In poverty, hunger and dirt,
　And still with a voice of dolorous pitch,
　She sang the song of the shirt!
　Sewing at once with a double thread,
　A shroud, as well as a shirt! "

Ever and anon the very soul is ready to
sing:

" Oh, land of rest for thee I sigh,
　When will the moment come,
　When I shall lay my armour by,
　And dwell in peace at home."

Over the main gate of Greenwood Cemetery were these words, "A Night's Rest on the
Way to the City of the New Jerusalem."
Thank God, death is the door to heaven, and
heaven is everlasting rest. Let us be cheered
and sustained by the blessed hope that there
remaineth a rest for the people of God—

" Where the wicked cease from troubling,
　And the weary are at rest."

Sometime since, I stood by the bed of a dying
boy. Half unconscious, as he was nearing the
end, he said: " I am tired and want to go

home." In a few moments he ended his brief visit to earth, and went to his heavenly home to rest forever. Well may we sing—

" One sweetly solemn thought comes to me o'er
    and o'er,
  I'm nearer my home to-day, than I have been
    before."

We love to believe heaven a place of intellectual activity. It is unreasonable to believe we shall have a glorified body, and not a glorified mind. Many fear that there will be no such thing as heavenly recognition. For my part, I do not expect to know less, but infinitely more in heaven. The three apostles immediately recognized Moses and Elias on the Mount of Transfiguration, though they had never before seen them. Rest assured, we shall know our deathless dead in a land where death is unknown. Many of us have a sufficient number of dead to make a heaven of our own. While we shall have glorified bodies, they will be bodies that may be recognized. Our personality will be preserved in heaven. With these eyes I expect to behold the King in His beauty, and my own loved ones. With these hands I hope to clasp hands with those who " once went sorrowing here." There will be many a family reunion in the Land of the Unsetting Sun. There we shall live forever with those we have "loved and lost a while."

Heaven will doubtless be a place of spiritual activity. Certainly, we shall worship there. With the angels of God we shall cry, "Holy, Holy, Lord God Almighty!" There our poor stammering tongues will be loosed. On earth our worship is poor and imperfect, but in heaven will swell the anthem note of perfected praise. With loud halleluiah and everlasting hosanna we will praise God from whom all blessings flow!

In that Better Land many of the dark providences of time will be explained, and all the mysteries of life will be solved in the light of a clearer day. Events that staggered and dumbfounded us will appear so simple and blessed that we will almost wonder why we did not thank God for them when they came. Why the lonely widow was left to battle alone; why the mother was taken and the little child left without a mother's love and care, will appear in the land where no clouds ever come. The meaning and mystery of our tears will be understood and justified, and we shall know that all things have worked together for good to those who loved God, and were the called according to His purpose.

The chief question concerning the heavenly kingdom is, who will be its subjects? We may well imagine the gates of this city are pearl, and its streets all gold, but who shall enter these gates, and walk the streets of the Celestial City, through the endless years? Only those who have been redeemed by His own precious blood will have a home in glory. There is no other name given under heaven by which we may enter through the gates into the city. His blood is our only hope of glory, for the blood of Jesus Christ His Son cleanses us from all sin. In his beatific vision John asked, "Who are these?" and prompt the response, "These are they who have come up out of great tribulation, and washed their robes and made them white in the blood of the Lamb." It was a blood-washed throng that he beheld. Only those will live with the Lord, who have been reconciled to God through the atoning blood of the Son of God. The redeemed only will live with the Redeemer.

We are persuaded that many will share the blessings of eternal happiness. The faithful of all ages will be there, for they shall come up from the North and the South, and from the East and the West, and sit down with Abraham and Isaac and Jacob in the Kingdom of heaven. It will be a mighty multitude that no man can number; yea, as the sands of the sea and the stars of the sky.

We know that Jesus will be there. Here we have only caught glimpses of His glory; but then, through riches of grace, we shall see Him face to face. We long to see others, but high above all, we long to see Him who died that we might shun hell and gain heaven. Yes, we shall see Him, and know Him, by the prints of the nails in His hands!

> " Jesus, the very thought of Thee
> With sweetness fills my breast;
> But sweeter far Thy face to see,
> And in Thy presence rest."

Whatever the disappointments, the trials of the present, or the forebodings of the future, we know the best is ahead, for heaven's ahead, and heaven is the best of all. How true, the tears and toils of the journey will seem as nothing when we reach the end of the way. Whatever our crosses, we shall soon lay them down at His blessed feet. Infinite comfort!

Everlasting consolation! "And there shall be no curse any more; and the throne of God and the Lamb shall be therein, and His servants shall do Him service. And they shall see His face; and His name shall be in their foreheads. And there shall be night no more, and they need no light of lamp; neither light of sun; for the Lord God shall give them light, and they shall reign forever and ever."

"They tell me of a city far up in the sky,
 I want to go there, I do,
 It is built in the land of the sweet by and by,
 I want to go there, don't you?"

Printed in the United States of America